Word of the Day 2017

HINKHOJ

notionpress.com

INDIA • SINGAPORE • MALAYSIA

Notion Press

Old No. 38, New No. 6
McNichols Road, Chetpet
Chennai - 600 031

First Published by Notion Press 2018
Copyright © HinKhoj 2018
All Rights Reserved.

ISBN 978-1-64249-712-0

INTRODUCTION

Dear Reader,

Do you think books are losing their essence and importance? Well to some extent YES. Reason is that everything is now available "JUST A CLICK AWAY". Let us come to the point.

The base of any language is based on its vast vocabulary. Now you will get words information online anytime, anywhere. How effectively you are using your vocabulary, reflects your deep knowledge of the language. It is rightly said that one can not remember everything until and unless it is repeated. You might have seen or read these words somewhere but the question remains the same - How many words have you remembered out of them?

This book "Word of the Day 2017" solves your problem. It is a collection of words which were there in news in the year 2017. How this book is different from others?

Meaning is easily available and sometimes you know them. But here, for the betterment of the users, pronunciation is given in Hindi. Not only this, you will get the Word type (category), Synonyms and Antonyms. You can easily associate yourself with the examples because you have already read them before. English is one of the major subject tested in all the competitive exams. But we want masses to be benefitted by this book. Not only for the students, who are appearing in various competitive exams, this book will be helpful for housewives, working people and school students also.

This book is brought to you by Hinkhoj.com which is already a well known online dictionary. Already we have got a lot of appreciation from our online users. You can get all these words from our website also. Now we are publishing this book which you can keep, carry and use anywhere, anytime. No doubt, it is our first venture in printed form but we are sure that we will get the same response which we received online. We will bring

"Word of the Day" series every year. Also, we appreciate feedbacks from our readers and promise to work on those suggestions in our next edition. So let's start working together.

The whole team of Hinkhoj, wishes you all the best for your future and committed to help you to achieve success.

January 2017

Date: 2017/01/01

WOD: *Pique*

Pronunciation: पीक

Type of word (Category): *Verb*

English meaning: *arouse (interest or curiosity)*

Hindi meaning: पैदा करना

Synonyms: *arouse, rouse, provoke, kindle*

Antonyms: *calm, soothe, subdue*

English Example: *Aditya Roy Kapur and Shraddha Kapoor's upcoming film 'Ok Jaanu' can pique their fan's interest in the romance drama.*

Hindi Example: आदित्य रॉय कपूर और श्रद्धा कपूर की आने वाली फिल्म 'ओके जानू' रोमांस नाटक में उनके प्रशंसकों की रूचि पैदा कर सकती है।

Date: 2017/01/02

WOD: *Enamored*

Pronunciation: एनैमर्ड

Type of word (Category): *Adjective*

English meaning: *have a liking or admiration for*

Hindi meaning: मोहित

Synonyms: *charmed, infatuated, smitten, captivated, enchanted*

Antonyms: *disliked, disenchanted, hated*

English Example: *Daddy Saif is so enamored by his baby's arrival that he has even changed his WhatsApp display picture.*

Hindi Example: पिता सैफ अपने बच्चे के आगमन से इतने मोहित है कि उन्होंने अपना व्हाट्सएप्प प्रदर्शित चित्र भी बदल दिया है।

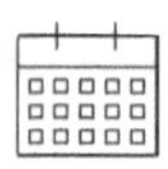

Date: 2017/01/03

WOD: *Compatriot*

Pronunciation: कम्पे-ट्रीअट

Type of word (Category): Noun

English meaning: a fellow citizen or national of a country

Hindi meaning: हमवतन

Synonyms: fellow countryman, countryman, fellow citizen, comrade

Antonyms: outsider, foreigner, stranger

English Example: Carlos Tevez is earning more than his compatriot Messi and become the highest earning footballer in the world.

Hindi Example: कार्लोस टेवेज अपने हमवतन मेस्सी की तुलना में अधिक कमाई और दुनिया में सबसे ज्यादा कमाई वाले फुटबॉलर बन गए हैं।

Date: 2017/01/04

WOD: *Usurer*

Pronunciation: यूशरर

Type of word (Category): Noun

English meaning: a person who lends money at unreasonably high rates of interest

Hindi meaning: सूदखोर

Synonyms: moneylender, banker, lender, loan shark

Antonyms: borrower, recipient, receiver

English Example: Due to the demonetisation and lack of bank loans, farmers are forced to take money from usurers.

Hindi Example: विमुद्रीकरण और बैंक ऋण में कमी के कारण, किसान सूदखोरों से पैसे लेने के लिए मजबूर हैं।

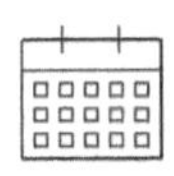 **Date: 2017/01/05**

WOD: *Frolic*

Pronunciation: फ्रालिक

Type of word (Category): Noun

English meaning: a playful and lively movement or activity

Hindi meaning: मस्ती

Synonyms: antic, caper, romp, revel, spree, merrymaking

Antonyms: work, bore, upset

English Example: BSF jawans welcomed New Year with dance, prayers and frolic.

Hindi Example: सीमा सुरक्षा बल के जवानों ने नृत्य, प्रार्थना और मस्ती के साथ नए साल का स्वागत किया।

Date: 2017/01/06

WOD: *Annals*

Pronunciation: ऐनल्ज़

Type of word (Category): Noun

English meaning: a record of events year by year

Hindi meaning: इतिहास

Synonyms: chronicle, history, record, journal

Antonyms: -

English Example: "Dhoni's achievements will remain forever in the annals of Indian cricket"; said BCCI CEO Rahul Johri.

Hindi Example: "धोनी की उपलब्धियाँ भारतीय क्रिकेट के इतिहास में हमेशा रहेंगी"; बीसीसीआई के मुख्य कार्यकारी अधिकारी राहुल जौहरी ने कहा।

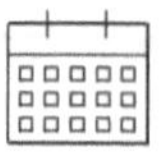 **Date: 2017/01/07**

WOD: *Etch*

Pronunciation: एच

Type of word (Category): *Verb*

English meaning: (of an experience, image, etc.) be permanently fixed in someone's memory

Hindi meaning: साफ़ झलकना

Synonyms: delineate, imprint, inscribe

Antonyms: neglect, confuse

English Example: Guru Gobind Singh's bravery etch in every Indian's heart: said PM Modi.

Hindi Example: गुरु गोबिंद सिंह की बहादुरी हर भारतीय के दिल में साफ़ झलकती है: प्रधानमंत्री मोदी ने कहा।

Date: 2017/01/08

WOD: *Plummet*

Pronunciation: प्लमिट

Type of word (Category): *Verb*

English meaning: fall or drop straight down at high speed

Hindi meaning: अचानक गिर जाना

Synonyms: plunge, fall, dive, tumble, decline

Antonyms: ascend, rise, climb, increase

English Example: Mild snowfall plummeted temperature in Himachal Pradesh.

Hindi Example: हल्के हिमपात से हिमाचल प्रदेश का तापमान अचानक गिर गया।

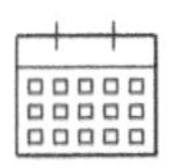 **Date: 2017/01/09**

WOD: *Expat*

Pronunciation: एक्स्पैट

Type of word (Category): Noun

English meaning: someone who does not live in their own country

Hindi meaning: प्रवासी

Synonyms: expatriate, immigrant, expatriation

Antonyms: citizen

English Example: Switzerland is the best country for expats to work in.

Hindi Example: स्विट्जरलैंड प्रवासियों के काम करने के लिए सबसे अच्छा देश है।

Date: 2017/01/10

WOD: *Stealth*

Pronunciation: स्टेल्थ

Type of word (Category): Noun

English meaning: movement that is quiet and careful in order not to be seen or heard, or secret action

Hindi meaning: चुपके से जानेवाला

Synonyms: secrecy, sneakiness, slyness, covertness

Antonyms: uncovering, detection

English Example: IIT-Madras scientists have developed stealth ships.

Hindi Example: आईआईटी-मद्रास के वैज्ञानिकों ने चुपके से जानेवाले जहाजों को विकसित किया है।

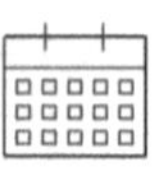 **Date: 2017/01/11**

WOD: *Fervour*

Pronunciation: फर्वर

Type of word (Category): Noun

English meaning: intense and passionate feeling

Hindi meaning: जोश

Synonyms: passion, excitement, intensity, zeal, enthusiasm

Antonyms: agony, boredom

English Example: Raees's song 'Udi Udi Jaye' adds festive fervour to Makar Sankranti.

Hindi Example: रईस का गीत 'उड़ी उड़ी जाए' मकर संक्रांति में उत्सवी जोश जोड़ता हैं।

Date: 2017/01/12

WOD: *Snub*

Pronunciation: स्नब

Type of word (Category): Verb

English meaning: rebuff, ignore, or spurn disdainfully

Hindi meaning: अनदेखा करके अपमानित करना

Synonyms: insult, slight, affront, humiliate, repulse

Antonyms: welcome, acknowledge, be friendly

English Example: Ravi Shastri snubbed Sourav Ganguly, hailed MS Dhoni.

Hindi Example: रवि शास्त्री ने सौरव गांगुली को अनदेखा कर अपमानित किया, महेंद्र सिंह धोनी की प्रंशसा की।

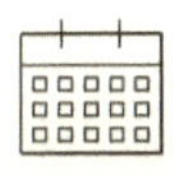

Date: 2017/01/13

WOD: *Promulgate*

Pronunciation: प्रामल्गेट

Type of word (Category): *Verb*

English meaning: *put (a law or decree) into effect by official proclamation*

Hindi meaning: लागू करना

Synonyms: *enact, implement, enforce, pass*

Antonyms: *cover, conceal*

English Example: *UK Sasikala urged Narendra Modi to promulgate ordinance for Jallikattu.*

Hindi Example: वीके शशिकला ने नरेंद्र मोदी से जल्लीकट्टू के लिए अध्यादेश लागू करने का आग्रह किया।

Date: 2017/01/14

WOD: *Berserk*

Pronunciation: ब-र्सर्क

Type of word (Category): *Adjective*

English meaning: *out of control with anger or excitement; wild or frenzied*

Hindi meaning: पागल

Synonyms: *mad, crazy, insane, frenzied, uncontrollable*

Antonyms: *normal, sane, rational*

English Example: *The crowd went berserk after seeing Big Boss 10 contestants Manu and Manveer in the mall.*

Hindi Example: भीड़ मॉल में बिग बॉस 10 के प्रतियोगियों मनु और मनवीर को देख कर पागल हो गयी।

Date: 2017/01/15

WOD: *Rescind*

Pronunciation: रि-सिन्ड

Type of word (Category):   *Verb*

English meaning: *revoke, cancel, or repeal (a law, order, or agreement)*

Hindi meaning: रद्द कर देना

Synonyms: *revoke, repeal, cancel, reverse, abolish, withdraw, nullify, overturn*

Antonyms: *allow, approve, establish, enact*

English Example: *Tricolour doormats: No visas, even the visas issued earlier would also be rescinded, Sushma Swaraj warned Amazon.*

Hindi Example: तिरंगा पायदान: वीजा नहीं, यहाँ तक कि पहले जारी किये वीजा भी रद्द कर देंगे, सुषमा स्वराज ने अमेज़न को चेतावनी दी।

Date: 2017/01/16

WOD: *Bonhomie*

Pronunciation: बॉनमी

Type of word (Category):   *Noun*

English meaning: *cheerful friendliness; geniality*

Hindi meaning: खुशमिजाजी

Synonyms: *geniality, congeniality, joviality, cheerfulness, affability*

Antonyms: *coldness, sulkiness*

English Example: *The bonhomie and the bond which Dhoni and Virat have will only help Virat to grow as a leade; said Anil Kumble.*

Hindi Example: खुशमिजाजी और मेल जो धोनी और विराट में है केवल विराट को एक नेता के रूप में विकसित करने में मदद करेगी; अनिल कुंबले ने कहा।

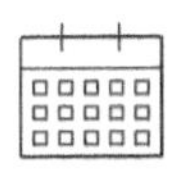 **Date: 2017/01/17**

WOD: *Cornerstone*

Pronunciation: कॉर्नस्टोन

Type of word (Category): Noun

English meaning: an important quality or feature on which a particular thing depends or is based

Hindi meaning: आधारशिला

Synonyms: foundation, basis, keystone, groundwork

Antonyms: abolish, avert, wreck

English Example: Virat Kohli and Kedar Jadhav's magnificent centuries were the cornerstone of India's win over England.

Hindi Example: विराट कोहली और केदार जाधव के शानदार शतक इंग्लैंड पर भारत की जीत की आधारशिला थे।

Date: 2017/01/18

WOD: *Figment*

Pronunciation: फिग्मन्ट

Type of word (Category): Noun

English meaning: a thing that someone believes to be real but that exists only in their imagination

Hindi meaning: मनगढ़ंत बात

Synonyms: fantasy, fiction, myth, fabrication

Antonyms: reality, fact, truth

English Example: Chennai to Bengaluru in 30 minutes! This is not a figment of imagination, but a proposed mode of transport.

Hindi Example: 30 मिनट में चेन्नई से बेंगलुरु! यह कल्पना की मनगढ़ंत बात नहीं है, बल्कि परिवहन का एक प्रस्तावित साधन है।

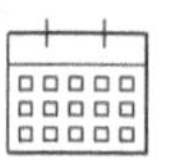 **Date: 2017/01/19**

WOD: *Envisage*

Pronunciation: एन्विज़िज

Type of word (Category):   *Verb*

English meaning: contemplate or conceive of as a possibility or a desirable future event

Hindi meaning: परिकल्पना करना

Synonyms: foresee, predict, forecast, foretell, anticipate, envision

Antonyms: unforeseen, unseen, withdrawn

English Example: Airbus envisages a future in which people are able to book flying taxis through an app.

Hindi Example: एयरबस एक ऐसे भविष्य की परिकल्पना करती है जिसमें लोग एप्प के माध्यम से उड़ने वाली टैक्सियों को बुक करने में सक्षम हो।

Date: 2017/01/20

WOD: *Vehemently*

Pronunciation: वीअमन्ट्ली

Type of word (Category):   *Adverb*

English meaning: in a forceful, passionate, or intense manner; with great feeling

Hindi meaning: ज़ोरदार ढंग से

Synonyms: furiously, violently, fiercely, intensely, ferociously

Antonyms: calmly, tranquilly, serenely, peacefully

English Example: WhatsApp has vehemently denied having a backdoor for governments in its encryption system.

Hindi Example: व्हाट्सएप्प ने ज़ोरदार ढंग से सरकारों के लिए अपनी एन्क्रिप्शन व्यवस्था में पीछे का द्वार होने से इनकार किया है।

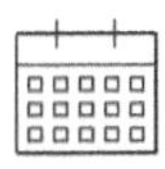 **Date: 2017/01/21**

WOD: *Raucous*

Pronunciation: रॉकस

Type of word (Category): Adjective

English meaning: making or constituting a disturbingly harsh and loud noise

Hindi meaning: भारी आवाज

Synonyms: harsh, screeching, husky, hoarse, strident

Antonyms: soft, dulcet, peaceful, quiet

English Example: The Cuttack crowd greeted Yuvraj Singh's century with raucous applaud.

Hindi Example: कटक भीड़ ने भारी आवाज में तालियाँ बजा कर युवराज सिंह के शतक का स्वागत किया।

Date: 2017/01/22

WOD: *Trample*

Pronunciation: ट्रैम्पल

Type of word (Category): Verb

English meaning: tread on and crush

Hindi meaning: कुचल देना

Synonyms: crush, squash, stamp, tread

Antonyms: assist, help, heal

English Example: For the protesters, Jallikattu is a fight for cultural heritage being trampled upon by biased decision makers.

Hindi Example: प्रदर्शनकारियों के लिए, जल्लीकट्टू सांस्कृतिक विरासत की एक लड़ाई है जो कि पक्षपातपूर्ण निर्णय निर्माताओं द्वारा कुचला जा रहा है।

Date: 2017/01/23

WOD: *Pivot*

Pronunciation: पिवट

Type of word (Category): Noun

English meaning: a person or thing that plays a central part in a situation or enterprise

Hindi meaning: केंद्रबिंदु

Synonyms: centre, central point, keystone, crux, cornerstone

Antonyms: border, edge, outskirt

English Example: Yuvraj Singh and MS Dhoni have been often the pivot of an Indian victory.

Hindi Example: युवराज सिंह और महेंद्र सिंह धोनी अक्सर भारतीय जीत के केंद्रबिंदु रह चुके हैं।

Date: 2017/01/24

WOD: *Procure*

Pronunciation: प्रो-क्युर

Type of word (Category): Verb

English meaning: obtain (something), especially with care or effort

Hindi meaning: प्राप्त करना

Synonyms: obtain, acquire, get, secure

Antonyms: lose, fail, give away

English Example: Last year, Gul Panag added one more feather in her cap by procuring her licence to fly.

Hindi Example: पिछले साल, गुल पनाग ने उड़ान भरने का लाइसेंस प्राप्त कर एक और सफलता हासिल की।

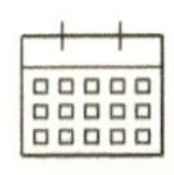 **Date: 2017/01/25**

WOD: *Deluge*

Pronunciation: डेल्यूज़

Type of word (Category): Noun

English meaning: a severe flood

Hindi meaning: बाढ़

Synonyms: flood, flash flood, torrent

Antonyms: drought, dearth

English Example: A deluge of people converged at Vadodara Station last night to catch a glimpse of Shah Rukh Khan.

Hindi Example: लोगों की बाढ़ कल रात वडोदरा स्टेशन पर शाहरुख खान की एक झलक पाने के लिए मिली।

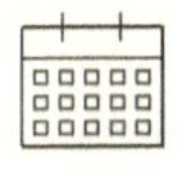 **Date: 2017/01/26**

WOD: *Bravura*

Pronunciation: ब्र-व्युर

Type of word (Category): Noun

English meaning: great technical skill and brilliance shown in a performance or activity

Hindi meaning: साहसपूर्ण प्रदर्शन

Synonyms: virtuoso, magnificent, outstanding, exceptional, excellent

Antonyms: normal, infirmity

English Example: The highlight of the new movie 'Kaabil' is Hrithik Roshan's bravura performance.

Hindi Example: नई फिल्म 'काबिल' का मुख्य आकर्षण रितिक रोशन का साहसपूर्ण प्रदर्शन है।

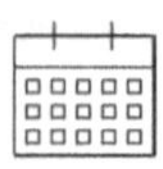 **Date: 2017/01/27**

WOD: *Staunch*

Pronunciation: स्टान्च

Type of word (Category): Adjective

English meaning: very loyal and committed in attitude

Hindi meaning: सच्चा

Synonyms: stalwart, loyal, faithful, trusty, committed, devoted, dedicated, dependable, reliable

Antonyms: disloyal, unfaithful, unreliable

English Example: Bihar attempted to form the world's longest human chain to show staunch support towards total prohibition of liquor.

Hindi Example: बिहार ने पूरी तरह से शराब निषेध के प्रति सच्चा समर्थन दिखाने के लिए दुनिया की सबसे लंबी मानव श्रृंखला बनाने का प्रयास किया।

Date: 2017/01/28

WOD: *Prowess*

Pronunciation: प्राउइस

Type of word (Category): Noun

English meaning: skill or expertise in a particular activity or field

Hindi meaning: कौशल

Synonyms: skill, expertise, experience, proficiency, capability

Antonyms: weakness, cowardice, inability

English Example: As the country celebrated its 68th Republic Day, the nation's military prowess was on showcase.

Hindi Example: जब देश ने अपना 68वां गणतंत्र दिवस मनाया, देश का सैन्य कौशल प्रदर्शन पर था।

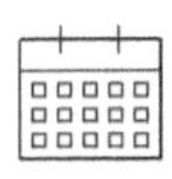
Date: 2017/01/29

WOD: *Tableau*

Pronunciation: टैब्लो

Type of word (Category): Noun

English meaning: a group of models or motionless figures representing a scene from a story or from history

Hindi meaning: झाँकी

Synonyms: picture, painting, representation, portrayal, illustration, image

Antonyms: -

English Example: A tableau displaying objectives and benefits of GST was also showcased during the 68th Republic Day parade.

Hindi Example: जीएसटी के उद्देश्यों और लाभों को प्रदर्शित करती झाँकी को भी 68वें गणतंत्र दिवस परेड के दौरान प्रदर्शित किया गया।

Date: 2017/01/30

WOD: *Bootlegger*

Pronunciation: बूट्लेगर

Type of word (Category): Noun

English meaning: someone who sells illegally made goods

Hindi meaning: शराब की तस्करी

Synonyms: moonshiner, vintner, tapster

Antonyms: -

English Example: Shahrukh Khan in his new movie 'Raees' played the role of bootlegger of the town.

Hindi Example: अपनी नई फिल्म 'रईस' में शाहरुख खान ने शराब की तस्करी करने वाले की भूमिका निभाई।

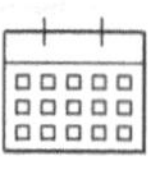 **Date: 2017/01/31**

WOD: *Vintage*

Pronunciation: विन्टिज

Type of word (Category):   Adjective

English meaning: denoting something from the past of high quality, especially something representing the best of its kind

Hindi meaning: श्रेष्ठ

Synonyms: high-quality, quality, superior, best

Antonyms: inferior, unimportant, minor

English Example: Roger Federer won his 18th major title after a vintage battle with Rafael Nadal.

Hindi Example: रोजर फेडरर ने राफेल नडाल के साथ एक श्रेष्ठ संघर्ष के बाद अपना 18वां प्रमुख खिताब जीता।

February 2017

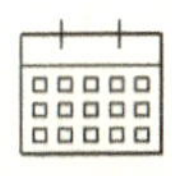 **Date: 2017/02/01**

WOD: *School*

Pronunciation: स्कूल

Type of word (Category):   Verb

English meaning: to train a person or animal to do something

Hindi meaning: प्रशिक्षित करना

Synonyms: educate, instruct

Antonyms: prevention, hindrance

English Example: Delhi's pizza delivery boys got schooled in traffic safety by cops.

Hindi Example: दिल्ली के पिज़्ज़ा डिलीवरी लड़कों को पुलिस द्वारा यातायात सुरक्षा में प्रशिक्षित किया गया।

 **Date: 2017/02/02**

WOD: *Custodian*

Pronunciation: क-स्टोडीअन

Type of word (Category):   Noun

English meaning: a person who has responsibility for taking care of or protecting something

Hindi meaning: संरक्षक

Synonyms: caretaker, guardian, superintendent, warden, protector

Antonyms: abuser, betrayer

English Example: The government is now seen as a trusted custodian of public money: Arun Jaitley said during Union Budget 2017.

Hindi Example: सरकार को अब जनता के पैसे का एक विश्वसनीय संरक्षक के रूप में देखा जाता है: अरुण जेटली ने केंद्रीय बजट 2017 के दौरान कहा।

📅 **Date: 2017/02/03**

WOD: *Plaudits*

Pronunciation: प्लॉडिट्स

Type of word (Category): Noun

English meaning: praise

Hindi meaning: शाबाशी

Synonyms: kudos, acclaim, congratulations, compliments, cheers

Antonyms: blame, criticism, flak

English Example: Though Yuzvendra Chahal got the plaudits for his superb bowling, the win over England was a combined team effort.

Hindi Example: हालांकि यजुवेंद्र चहल को उनकी शानदार गेंदबाजी के लिए शाबाशी मिली, इंग्लैंड पर जीत एक संयुक्त टीम की मेहनत थी।

📅 **Date: 2017/02/04**

WOD: *Issuance*

Pronunciation: इशूअन्स

Type of word (Category): Noun

English meaning: the action of supplying or distributing something, especially for official purposes

Hindi meaning: जारी करना

Synonyms: issue, circulation, release, distribution

Antonyms: take, block, freeze

English Example: Kuwait has suspended the issuance of visas for nationals of Syria, Iraq, Pakistan, Afghanistan and Iran.

Hindi Example: कुवैत ने सीरिया, इराक, पाकिस्तान, अफगानिस्तान और ईरान के नागरिकों के लिए वीजा जारी करना रोक दिया है।

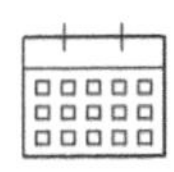

Date: 2017/02/05

WOD: *Fashionista*

Pronunciation: फैशानिस्टा

Type of word (Category):   Noun

English meaning: *a devoted follower of fashion*

Hindi meaning: फैशन का शौकीन

Synonyms: *fashion monger, trend-setter, follower of the latest fashions*

Antonyms: -

English Example: *Fashionista Sonam Kapoor has launched a series of emoji stickers, featuring herself.*

Hindi Example: फैशन की शौकीन सोनम कपूर ने खुद को दिखाते हुए इमोजी स्टिकरों की एक श्रृंखला शुरू की है।

Date: 2017/02/06

WOD: *Gaffe*

Pronunciation: गैफ

Type of word (Category):   Noun

English meaning: *an unintentional act or remark causing embarrassment to its originator; a blunder*

Hindi meaning: भारी भूल

Synonyms: *blunder, mistake, error, blooper, indiscretion*

Antonyms: *correction*

English Example: *Steve Harvey mentioned his 2015 gaffe before announcing the name of Miss Universe 2017.*

Hindi Example: स्टीव हार्वे ने मिस यूनिवर्स 2017 के नाम की घोषणा से पहले अपने 2015 की भारी भूल का उल्लेख किया।

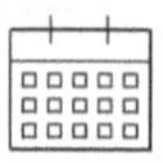 **Date: 2017/02/07**

WOD: *Clout*

Pronunciation: क्लाउट

Type of word (Category): Noun

English meaning: influence or power, especially in politics or business

Hindi meaning: प्रभाव

Synonyms: influence, power, control, dominance, mastery

Antonyms: powerlessness, weakness

English Example: India's clout in cricket is set to shrink.

Hindi Example: क्रिकेट में भारत का प्रभाव कम होना तय है।

Date: 2017/02/08

WOD: *Songstress*

Pronunciation: साँगस्ट्रिस

Type of word (Category): Noun

English meaning: a skilled female singer

Hindi meaning: गायिका

Synonyms: songster, singer, vocalist

Antonyms: -

English Example: The 24-year-old songstress, Miley Cyrus, posted a picture on Instagram of Lakshmi Puja at her home.

Hindi Example: 24-वर्षीय गायिका, माइली साइरस, ने अपने घर पर लक्ष्मी पूजा की तस्वीर इंस्टाग्राम पर पोस्ट की।

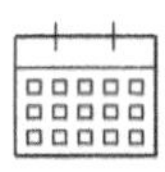 **Date: 2017/02/09**

WOD: *Plight*

Pronunciation: फ्लाइट

Type of word (Category):   Noun

English meaning: a dangerous, difficult, or otherwise unfortunate situation

Hindi meaning: दुर्दशा

Synonyms: dilemma, difficulty, predicament, trouble

Antonyms: good fortune, boon, advantage

English Example: Hrithik understood the plight of the blind man during the filming of the movie "Kaabil" and pledged to donate his eyes.

Hindi Example: ऋतिक ने फिल्म 'काबिल'; की शूटिंग के दौरान अंधे व्यक्ति की दुर्दशा को समझा और अपनी आँखें दान करने का वचन दिया।

Date: 2017/02/10

WOD: *Maverick*

Pronunciation: मैवरिक

Type of word (Category):   Adjective

English meaning: unorthodox

Hindi meaning: अपरंपरागत

Synonyms: unorthodox, individualist, nonconformist, eccentric

Antonyms: conformist, orthodox

English Example: Silican Valley maverick entrepreneur Elon Musk hinted at opening a unit of Tesla in India.

Hindi Example: सिलिकॉन वैली के अपरंपरागत व्यवसायी एलोन मस्क ने भारत में टेस्ला की एक इकाई खोलने का संकेत दिया।

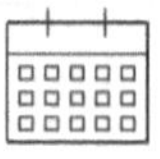 **Date: 2017/02/11**

WOD: *Honcho*

Pronunciation: हॉन्चो

Type of word (Category): Noun

English meaning: a leader or manager; the person in charge

Hindi meaning: नेता

Synonyms: boss, chief, leader, head

Antonyms: aide, employee, attendant

English Example: AIDMK honcho joined O Panneerselvam camp.

Hindi Example: अन्नाद्रमुक नेता ओ पनीरसेल्वम गुट में शामिल हुए।

Date: 2017/02/12

WOD: *Consecutive*

Pronunciation: कन्सेक्यटिव

Type of word (Category): Adjective

English meaning: following each other continuously

Hindi meaning: लगातार

Synonyms: continuous, successive, uninterrupted, sequent, constant

Antonyms: discontinuous, broken, concurrent, intermittent

English Example: Virat Kohli became the first batsman to score double centuries in four consecutive Test series.

Hindi Example: विराट कोहली लगातार चार टेस्ट मैचों की सीरीज में दोहरा शतक बनाने वाले पहले बल्लेबाज बन गए।

Date: 2017/02/13

WOD: *Folklore*

Pronunciation: फोक्ल़ॉर

Type of word (Category):   Noun

English meaning: the traditional beliefs, customs, and stories of a community, passed through the generations by word of mouth

Hindi meaning: पौराणिक कथा

Synonyms: mythology, lore, oral history, tradition, fables, myths, legends

Antonyms: fact, reality, truth

English Example: Urvashi Kaur's collection in Lakmé Fashion Week was hugely inspired by the Indian folklore.

Hindi Example: लक्मे फैशन वीक में उर्वशी कौर का संग्रह भारतीय पौराणिक कथाओं से बहुत अधिक प्रेरित था।

Date: 2017/02/14

WOD: *Cater*

Pronunciation: केटर

Type of word (Category):   Verb

English meaning: provide with what is needed or required

Hindi meaning: आवश्यकताओं का ध्यान रखना

Synonyms: provide, serve, supply, purvey, provision, gratify

Antonyms: deprive, devoid

English Example: The BHIM app will now cater to almost 100% smartphone users in the country with the launch on iOS platform.

Hindi Example: भीम एप्लिकेशन अब आईओएस प्लेटफॉर्म पर लांच होने के साथ देश के लगभग 100% स्मार्टफोन उपभोक्ताओं की आवश्यकताओं का ध्यान रखेगा।

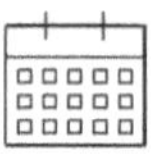 **Date: 2017/02/15**

WOD: *Adage*

Pronunciation: ऐडिज

Type of word (Category):   Noun

English meaning: a proverb or short statement expressing a general truth

Hindi meaning: कहावत

Synonyms: proverb, dictum, maxim, saying

Antonyms: -

English Example: A believer of the old adage, Indian skipper Virat Kohli on Monday lauded his bowlers.

Hindi Example: पुरानी कहावत के समर्थक, भारतीय क्रिकेट टीम के कप्तान विराट कोहली ने सोमवार को अपने गेंदबाजों की सराहना की।

Date: 2017/02/16

WOD: *Precedent*

Pronunciation: प्रेसिडन्ट

Type of word (Category):   Noun

English meaning: an earlier event or action that is regarded as an example or guide to be considered in subsequent similar circumstances

Hindi meaning: मिसाल

Synonyms: model, exemplar, example, paradigm

Antonyms: -

English Example: ISRO set a new precedent by launching a record 104 satellites in a single mission.

Hindi Example: इसरो ने एक ही मिशन में रिकार्ड 104 उपग्रहों को छोड़ कर एक नई मिसाल कायम की।

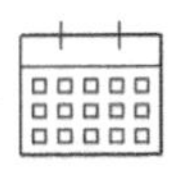

Date: 2017/02/17

WOD: *Swag*

Pronunciation: स्वैग

Type of word (Category): Noun

English meaning: valuable goods

Hindi meaning: बहुमूल्य सामान

Synonyms: booty, prize

Antonyms: -

English Example: iPhone is no more a swag now.

Hindi Example: आईफ़ोन अब कोई बहुमूल्य सामान नहीं रहा है।

Date: 2017/02/18

WOD: *Rig*

Pronunciation: रिग

Type of word (Category): Verb

English meaning: to arrange dishonestly for the result of something, for example an election, to be changed

Hindi meaning: हेर फेर करना

Synonyms: alter, cheat, furnish, fix, manipulate

Antonyms: unrig, disrobe

English Example: Rohan Mehra said Bigg Boss 10 was rigged, shared video on Twitter.

Hindi Example: रोहन मेहरा ने कहा कि बिग बॉस 10 में हेर-फेर की गई थी, ट्विटर पर वीडियो शेयर की।

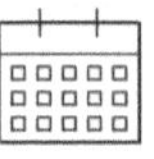 **Date: 2017/02/19**

WOD: *Rink*

Pronunciation: रिंक

Type of word (Category):   Noun

English meaning: an enclosed area of ice for skating, ice hockey, or curling

Hindi meaning: बर्फ़ का मैदान

Synonyms: ice field, skating rink, arena, ring

Antonyms: -

English Example: India's first women's ice hockey team was happy to participate on a professional rink for the first time last year.

Hindi Example: भारत की पहली महिला आइस हॉकी टीम पिछले साल पहली बार एक पेशेवर बर्फ़ के मैदान पर भाग ले कर खुश थी।

Date: 2017/02/20

WOD: *Warrant*

Pronunciation: वॉरन्ट

Type of word (Category):   Verb

English meaning: officially affirm or guarantee

Hindi meaning: आश्वासन देना

Synonyms: guarantee, affirm, swear, promise, vow, pledge

Antonyms: break, breach

English Example: The 59th Grammy Awards warranted Grammy glory for two Indian tabla artistes.

Hindi Example: 59वें ग्रैमी पुरस्कार ने दो भारतीय तबला कलाकारों को ग्रैमी यश देने का आश्वासन दिया।

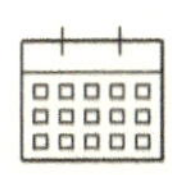 **Date: 2017/02/21**

WOD: *Dormant*

Pronunciation: डॉ-र्मन्ट

Type of word (Category): Adjective

English meaning: (of a volcano) temporarily inactive

Hindi meaning: निष्क्रिय

Synonyms: asleep, sleeping, slumbering, resting, reposing, drowsing

Antonyms: awake, active

English Example: After lying dormant for 150 years, India's only live volcano erupted again.

Hindi Example: 150 साल से निष्क्रिय पड़े होने के बाद, भारत का एकमात्र जीवित ज्वालामुखी फिर से फूट पड़ा।

Date: 2017/02/22

WOD: *Rake*

Pronunciation: रेक

Type of word (Category): Verb

English meaning: draw or drag (something) through something with a sweeping movement

Hindi meaning: इकट्ठा करना

Synonyms: make, collect, pull, draw,

Antonyms: decline, fall back

English Example: Britons and bowlers raked in the riches in this IPL auction.

Hindi Example: ब्रिटेनवासियों और गेंदबाजों ने इस आईपीएल नीलामी में धन इकट्ठा किया।

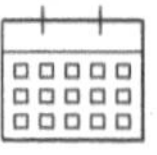

Date: 2017/02/23

WOD: *Infringement*

Pronunciation: इन्फ्रिन्ज्मन्ट

Type of word (Category):   Noun

English meaning: the action of breaking the terms of a law, agreement, etc.

Hindi meaning: उल्लंघन

Synonyms: contravention, violation, breach, breaking, transgression

Antonyms: obedience, observance, conformity

English Example: A lawsuit was filed against 'Rangoon' maker Vishal Bhardwaj on grounds of copyright infringement.

Hindi Example: कॉपीराइट उल्लंघन के विषय पर 'रंगून' निर्माता विशाल भारद्वाज के खिलाफ एक मुकदमा दायर किया गया।

Date: 2017/02/24

WOD: *Cannabis*

Pronunciation: कैनबिस

Type of word (Category):   Noun

English meaning: a tall plant with a stiff upright stem, divided serrated leaves, and glandular hairs (It is used to produce hemp fibre and as a psychotropic drug)

Hindi meaning: भांग

Synonyms: marijuana, hashish, bhang, ganja, sinsemilla

Antonyms: -

English Example: Thandai, a drink made with cannabis, almonds and milk, is drunk and distributed on Mahashivratri.

Hindi Example: ठंडाई, एक पेय जो कि भांग, बादाम और दूध के साथ बनाया जाता है, महाशिवरात्रि पर पिया और वितरित किया जाता है।

 **Date: 2017/02/25**

WOD: *Effluent*

Pronunciation: एफ्लूअन्ट

Type of word (Category): Noun

English meaning: liquid waste or sewage discharged into a river or the sea

Hindi meaning: गन्दा पानी

Synonyms: outflowing, effusive, pollutant, wastewater

Antonyms: -

English Example: Shut shops if you can't treat effluents, SC warned polluting industries.

Hindi Example: दुकानों को बंद करो अगर आप गंदे पानी का उपाय नहीं कर सकते, सुप्रीम कोर्ट ने प्रदूषण फैलाने वाले उद्योगों को चेतावनी दी।

Date: 2017/02/26

WOD: *Poop*

Pronunciation: पूप

Type of word (Category): Noun

English meaning: up-to-date or inside information

Hindi meaning: जानकारी

Synonyms: detail, information, instruction

Antonyms: -

English Example: This website gives you the latest poop direct from Hollywood.

Hindi Example: यह वेबसाइट आपको सीधे हॉलीवुड से नई जानकारी देती है।

Date: 2017/02/27

WOD: Monetary

Pronunciation: मानटेरी

Type of word (Category):   Adjective

English meaning: relating to money or currency

Hindi meaning: आर्थिक

Synonyms: financial, fiscal, pecuniary, economic, budgetary, capital

Antonyms: -

English Example: Gautam Gambhir extended monetary support to boxer Dingko Singh for his cancer treatment.

Hindi Example: गौतम गंभीर ने बॉक्सर डिंग्को सिंह को उनके कैंसर के इलाज के लिए आर्थिक सहायता दी।

Date: 2017/02/28

WOD: Usher

Pronunciation: अशर

Type of word (Category):   Noun

English meaning: a person who shows people to their seats, especially in a cinema or theatre or at a wedding

Hindi meaning: प्रवेशक

Synonyms: attendant, escort, guide, doorkeeper, commissionaire, aide

Antonyms: -

English Example: Shah Rukh Khan said that he got his first earning by working as an usher in Pankaj Udhas concert.

Hindi Example: शाहरुख खान ने कहा कि उन्हें पंकज उधास के संगीत कार्यक्रम में एक प्रवेशक के रूप में काम करके अपनी पहली कमाई मिली थी।

March 2017

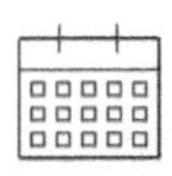

Date: 2017/03/01

WOD: *Render*

Pronunciation: रेन्डर

Type of word (Category): Noun

English meaning: to give something such as a service, a personal opinion or expression, or a performance of a song or poem, etc. to people

Hindi meaning: प्रस्तुत करना

Synonyms: give, deliver, provide, present, represent

Antonyms: take, conceal, hold, keep

English Example: Sara Bareilles rendered the song at the 89th Academy Awards ceremony in memory of all the departed souls including Om Puri.

Hindi Example: सारा बरेइलेस ने 89वें अकादमी पुरस्कार समारोह में ओम पुरी सहित सभी दिवंगत आत्माओं की याद में गाना प्रस्तुत किया।

Date: 2017/03/02

WOD: *Revamp*

Pronunciation: रीवैम्प

Type of word (Category): Verb

English meaning: give new and improved form, structure, or appearance to

Hindi meaning: पुनर्निर्माण करना

Synonyms: renovate, redecorate, rebuild, reconstruct, make over, improve, upgrade

Antonyms: damage, destroy, disfigure, abolish

English Example: An iconic Nokia phone 3310 is revamped with added battery life and new features.

Hindi Example: प्रतिष्ठित नोकिया फोन 3310 का अतिरिक्त बैटरी लाइफ और नई सुविधाओं के साथ पुनर्निर्माण किया गया है।

📅 **Date: 2017/03/03**

WOD: *Staggering*

Pronunciation: स्टैगरिंग

Type of word (Category): Adjective

English meaning: so surprisingly impressive as to stun or overwhelm, very shocking and surprising

Hindi meaning: चौंका देने वाला

Synonyms: overwhelming, amazing, astonishing, extraordinary, astounding

Antonyms: unremarkable, uninspiring, normal, uninteresting, unsurprising

English Example: Jitu Rai's staggering comeback helped him to win gold medal in 50m pistol event in the ISSF World Cup.

Hindi Example: जीतू राय की चौंका देने वाली वापसी ने आईएसएसएफ विश्व कप में 50 मीटर पिस्टल स्पर्धा में उसे स्वर्ण पदक जीतने में मदद की।

📅 **Date: 2017/03/04**

WOD: *Dissent*

Pronunciation: डिसेन्ट

Type of word (Category): Noun

English meaning: a strong difference of opinion on a particular subject, especially about an official suggestion or plan or a popular belief

Hindi meaning: असहमति

Synonyms: disagreement, argument, dispute, contention, disapproval, objection

Antonyms: assent, agreement, consent, assent

English Example: President Pranab Mukherjee on Thursday said that there must be space for legitimate criticism and dissent.

Hindi Example: गुरुवार को राष्ट्रपति प्रणब मुखर्जी ने कहा कि वैध आलोचना और असहमति के लिए हमेशा स्थान होना चाहिए।

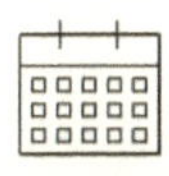 **Date: 2017/03/05**

WOD: *Content*

Pronunciation: कन्टेन्ट

Type of word (Category): Adjective

English meaning: in a state of peaceful happiness, satisfied with what one is or has; not wanting more or anything else

Hindi meaning: संतुष्ट

Synonyms: satisfied, pleased, fulfilled, happy, joyous

Antonyms: discontent, dissatisfied, depressed, discontented

English Example: Sir Patrick Stewart is feeling content about saying good bye to X-Men series.

Hindi Example: सर पैट्रिक स्टीवर्ट एक्स-मेन श्रृंखला को अलविदा कहते हुए संतुष्ट महसूस कर रहे हैं।

Date: 2017/03/06

WOD: *Susceptible*

Pronunciation: ससेप्टबल

Type of word (Category): Adjective

English meaning: likely or liable to be influenced or harmed by a particular thing

Hindi meaning: आसानी से प्रभावित होने वाला

Synonyms: an easy target for, easily moved, liable to, prone to

Antonyms: insusceptible, unresponsive, resistant, resisting

English Example: Pooja Bhatt agrees that being the daughter of an alcoholic makes you more susceptible to be an alcoholic.

Hindi Example: पूजा भट्ट मानती है कि एक शराबी की बेटी होने के नाते आप अधिक आसानी से प्रभावित हो कर एक शराबी बन जाते हैं।

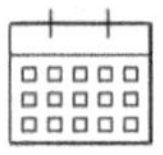

Date: 2017/03/07

WOD: *Fraternity*

Pronunciation: फ्रटर्निटी

Type of word (Category): Noun

English meaning: a group of people sharing a common profession or interests

Hindi meaning: बिरादरी

Synonyms: society, association, club, guild, group

Antonyms: –

English Example: The film fraternity is showering their blessings on Karan Johar and his two kids.

Hindi Example: फिल्म बिरादरी करण जौहर और उनके दोनों बच्चों पर अपने आशीर्वादों की वर्षा कर रही है।

Date: 2017/03/08

WOD: *Decommission*

Pronunciation: डीकमिशन

Type of word (Category): Verb

English meaning: withdraw (something, especially weapons or military equipment) from service

Hindi meaning: सेवा मुक्त करना

Synonyms: deactivate, demilitarize, demobilize

Antonyms: introduce

English Example: INS Viraat was decommissioned on Monday after serving the Indian Navy for nearly three decades.

Hindi Example: लगभग तीन दशकों तक भारतीय नौसेना की सेवा करने के बाद आईएनएस विराट को सोमवार को सेवा मुक्त कर दिया गया।

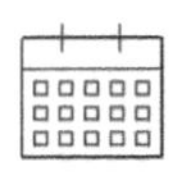 **Date: 2017/03/09**

WOD: *Lambast*

Pronunciation: लम-बासठ

Type of word (Category): *Verb*

English meaning: *criticize (someone or something) harshly*

Hindi meaning: बुरी तरह से फटकारना

Synonyms: *scold, criticize, attack, lash, rebuke*

Antonyms: *praise, uphold, compliment, laud, applaud*

English Example: *Kohli lambasted Australian skipper for not following DRS protocols.*

Hindi Example: डीआरएस प्रोटोकॉल का पालन नहीं करने के लिए कोहली ने ऑस्ट्रेलियाई कप्तान को बुरी तरह से फटकारा।

Date: 2017/03/10

WOD: *Parity*

Pronunciation: पै-रिटि

Type of word (Category): *Noun*

English meaning: *the state or condition of being equal, especially as regards status or pay*

Hindi meaning: समानता

Synonyms: *equality, equivalence, uniformity, sameness, correspondence*

Antonyms: *inequality, disproportion, diversity, gap*

English Example: *A small girl's statue in front of Wall Street bull is intended to mark International Women's Day is for gender parity.*

Hindi Example: वॉल स्ट्रीट बैल के सामने एक छोटी लड़की की मूर्ति का उद्देश्य अंतर्राष्ट्रीय महिला दिवस पर लिंग समानता चिन्हित करना है।

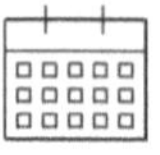

WOD: *Nemesis*

Pronunciation: नेम्इ-सिस

Type of word (Category): Noun

English meaning: a downfall caused by an inescapable agent

Hindi meaning: अभिशाप

Synonyms: torment, bane, curse, jinx

Antonyms: advantage

English Example: Bhagyashree's decision to only work with her husband Himalaya proved to be her nemesis.

Hindi Example: भाग्यश्री का सिर्फ अपने पति हिमालय के साथ काम करने का निर्णय उसके लिए अभिशाप साबित हुई।

Date: 2017/03/12

WOD: *Festivity*

Pronunciation: फ़ेस्टि-व़ुइटि

Type of word (Category): Noun

English meaning: the celebration of something in a joyful and exuberant way

Hindi meaning: उत्सव

Synonyms: celebration, revelry, feast, merrymaking, gaiety

Antonyms: gloom, sadness, unhappiness, misery

English Example: Thousands of devotees gather in the city to watch the "Lathmar Holi" festivities in Radha Rani temple, Barsana.

Hindi Example: बरसाना के राधा रानी मंदिर में "लाठमार होली" उत्सव देखने के लिए हजारों भक्त शहर में इकट्ठा होते हैं।

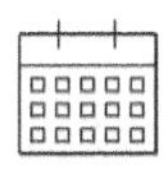 **Date: 2017/03/13**

WOD: *Gaiety*

Pronunciation: गेइटि

Type of word (Category): Noun

English meaning: the state or quality of being light-hearted or cheerful

Hindi meaning: प्रसन्नता

Synonyms: cheerfulness, cheer, light-heartedness, happiness, joy, joyfulness

Antonyms: unhappiness, sadness, depression

English Example: Holi is celebrated with fervour and gaiety in all over the country.

Hindi Example: पूरे देश में होली को जोश और प्रसन्नता से मनाया जाता है।

Date: 2017/03/14

WOD: *Moniker*

Pronunciation: मॉ-नि-कर

Type of word (Category): Noun

English meaning: a person's name, especially a nickname

Hindi meaning: उपनाम

Synonyms: nickname, title, name, label

Antonyms: -

English Example: Jackie Shroff earned the 'dada' moniker in the Teen Batti chawl.

Hindi Example: जैकी श्रॉफ ने तीन बत्ती चॉल में 'दादा' उपनाम प्राप्त किया था।

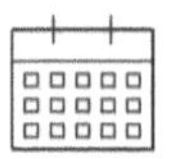 **Date: 2017/03/15**

WOD: *Rendition*

Pronunciation: रेन-डिशन

Type of word (Category): *Noun*

English meaning: *a performance or interpretation especially of a dramatic role or piece of music, a visual representation or reproduction*

Hindi meaning: प्रस्तुतीकरण

Synonyms: *depiction, portrayal, representation, delineation*

Antonyms: -

English Example: *Alia Bhatt and Varun Dhawan are back with a soulful rendition 'Humsafar' song for their film Badrinath Ki Dulhaniya.*

Hindi Example: आलिया भट्ट और वरुण धवन अपनी फिल्म बद्रीनाथ की दुल्हनिया के लिए एक भावपूर्ण प्रस्तुतीकरण 'हमसफ़र' गीत के साथ वापस आ रहे हैं।

Date: 2017/03/16

WOD: *Swear in*

Pronunciation: स्वे-र इन

Type of word (Category): *Verb*

English meaning: *take (an oath), make a solemn statement or promise undertaking to do something affirming that something is the case*

Hindi meaning: शपथ लेना

Synonyms: *promise, vow, oath, affirm, pledge, declare*

Antonyms: *disprove, deny, distrust, waive*

English Example: *Manohar Parrikar sworn in as Chief Minister of Goa.*

Hindi Example: मनोहर परिकर ने गोवा के मुख्यमंत्री के रूप में शपथ ली।

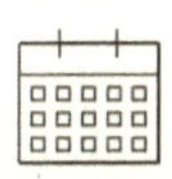 **Date: 2017/03/17**

WOD: *Miscreant*

Pronunciation: मिस्क्रीअन्ट

Type of word (Category):   *Noun*

English meaning: *a person who has done something wrong or unlawful*

Hindi meaning: बदमाश

Synonyms: *criminal, culprit, wrongdoer, offender, villain, lawbreaker*

Antonyms: *hero, innocent, pious, godly*

English Example: *The miscreants set on fire the set of Sanjay Leela Bhansali's film 'Padmavati' near Kolhapur.*

Hindi Example: कोल्हापुर के पास बदमाशों ने संजय लीला भंसाली की फिल्म 'पद्मावती' के सेट को जला दिया।

Date: 2017/03/18

WOD: *Shroud*

Pronunciation: श्राउड

Type of word (Category):   *Verb*

English meaning: *cover or envelop so as to conceal from view*

Hindi meaning: छिपाना

Synonyms: *cover, conceal, hide, mask, disguise*

Antonyms: *expose, uncover, discover, show*

English Example: *Baahubali 2 trailer is released but why Kattappa killed Baahubali still remains shrouded in mystery.*

Hindi Example: बाहुबली 2 ट्रेलर रिलीज़ हो गया है, लेकिन कट्टप्पा ने बाहुबली को क्यों मारा रहस्य अभी भी छिपा हुआ है।

📅 **Date: 2017/03/19**

WOD: *Hiatus*

Pronunciation: हाई-एटस

Type of word (Category):   Noun

English meaning: a pause or break in continuity in a sequence or activity

Hindi meaning: अंतराल

Synonyms: break, gap, interval, pause, interlude

Antonyms: continuation, concluding, continuity

English Example: After a hiatus of over a decade the popular show, Sarabhai vs Sarabhai, will return as a web series.

Hindi Example: एक दशक से अधिक अंतराल के बाद लोकप्रिय शो, साराभाई वर्सस साराभाई, एक वेब श्रृंखला के रूप में वापिस लौटेगा।

📅 **Date: 2017/03/20**

WOD: *Debacle*

Pronunciation: डी-बॉकल

Type of word (Category):   Noun

English meaning: a sudden and ignominious failure, a sudden violent event that brings about great loss or destruction

Hindi meaning: असफलता

Synonyms: fiasco, failure, collapse, disaster, downfall

Antonyms: achievement, success, victory, accomplishment

English Example: Raj Babbar offered to resign from the post of UP Congress chief after the poll debacle.

Hindi Example: राज बब्बर ने चुनाव में असफलता के बाद यूपी कांग्रेस प्रमुख के पद से इस्तीफा देने की पेशकश की।

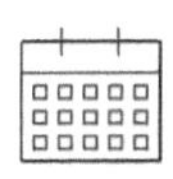 **Date: 2017/03/21**

WOD: *Firebrand*

Pronunciation: फायरब्रेन्ड

Type of word (Category): Noun

English meaning: a person who is very passionate about a particular cause

Hindi meaning: तेजतर्रार

Synonyms: troublemaker, instigator, provoker, radical, revolutionary

Antonyms: peacemaker, soother, calmer

English Example: Yogi Adityanath, the Chief Minister of UP, is a politician with a "firebrand Hindutva" image.

Hindi Example: योगी आदित्यनाथ, यूपी के मुख्यमंत्री, एक "तेजतर्रार हिंदुत्व" छवि वाले राजनेता हैं।

Date: 2017/03/22

WOD: *Astounding*

Pronunciation: अस्टा-उन्डिंग

Type of word (Category): Adjective

English meaning: surprisingly impressive or notable

Hindi meaning: चौंका देने वाला

Synonyms: amazing, astonishing, surprising, breathtaking, striking, impressive, bewildering, stunning

Antonyms: boring, dull, unimpressive, unremarkable

English Example: Federer won his 25th Masters Series title and a 90th career trophy by his astounding performances.

Hindi Example: फेडरर ने अपने चौंका देने वाले प्रदर्शन से अपना 25वां मास्टर्स सीरीज़ ख़िताब और कैरियर की 90वीं ट्रॉफी जीती।

📅 **Date: 2017/03/23**

WOD: *Dub*

Pronunciation: डब

Type of word (Category): *Verb*

English meaning: *give an unofficial name or nickname to*

Hindi meaning: नाम देना

Synonyms: *nickname, call, name, give a name, label, christen, term, tag, describe as*

Antonyms: *-*

English Example: *Australian media on Tuesday dubbed India captain Virat Kohli as Donald Trump of world sport.*

Hindi Example: ऑस्ट्रेलियाई मीडिया ने मंगलवार को भारतीय कप्तान विराट कोहली को खेल की दुनिया का डोनाल्ड ट्रम्प नाम दिया।

📅 **Date: 2017/03/24**

WOD: *Altercation*

Pronunciation: ऑः-ल्टॅ-केर्शॅन

Type of word (Category): *Noun*

English meaning: *a noisy argument or disagreement, especially in public*

Hindi meaning: झड़प

Synonyms: *argument, quarrel, squabble, fight, disagreement, dispute, contention, clash*

Antonyms: *agreement, harmony, accord, unity*

English Example: *Sunil Grover may quit Kapil Sharma's show after an altercation with Kapil.*

Hindi Example: कपिल के साथ झड़प के बाद सुनील ग्रोवर कपिल शर्मा के शो को छोड़ सकते हैं।

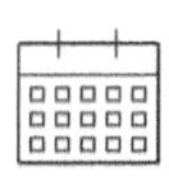 **Date: 2017/03/25**

WOD: *Absenteeism*

Pronunciation: ऐब्सं-टी-इज़म

Type of word (Category):   Noun

English meaning: the practice of regularly staying away from work or school without good reason

Hindi meaning: अनुपस्थिति

Synonyms: absence, nonattendance, skipping, non appearance

Antonyms: attendance, presence, alertness, attending

English Example: PM Modi said that he will not tolerate absenteeism of BJP MPs in Parliament any more.

Hindi Example: प्रधान मंत्री मोदी ने कहा कि वह संसद में भाजपा सांसदों की अनुपस्थिति को और अधिक सहन नहीं करेंगे।

Date: 2017/03/26

WOD: *Notch*

Pronunciation: नॉच

Type of word (Category):   Noun

English meaning: an imaginary point or position in a system of comparing values, a point or degree in a scale

Hindi meaning: स्तर

Synonyms: step, level, rung, point, mark, measure, grade, gradation, stage

Antonyms: -

English Example: Indian Idol Season 9 contestants have entertained everybody with their top notch singing and performances.

Hindi Example: इंडियन आइडल सीजन 9 प्रतियोगियों ने अपने शीर्ष स्तर के गायन और प्रदर्शन से सभी का मनोरंजन किया है।

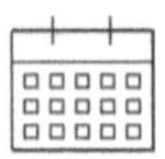

WOD: *Tenacious*

Pronunciation: टनै-सियस

Type of word (Category): Adjective

English meaning: persisting in existence, keeping an opinion in a determined way

Hindi meaning: दृढ

Synonyms: persistent, determined, strong-willed, resolute, firm, obstinate

Antonyms: loose, slack, irresolute, weak

English Example: Radhakishan Damani, a tenacious stock broker and entrepreneur, joined top 20 billionaires list after D-Mart's stellar performance.

Hindi Example: राधाकिशन दमानी, एक दृढ़ शेयर दलाल और उद्यमी, डी-मार्ट के शानदार प्रदर्शन के बाद शीर्ष 20 अरबपतियों की सूची में शामिल हो गए।

Date: 2017/03/28

WOD: *Engross*

Pronunciation: इन्ग्रोस

Type of word (Category): Verb

English meaning: absorb all the attention or interest of

Hindi meaning: ध्यान खींचना

Synonyms: absorb, preoccupy, engage, fascinate, grip, hold, interest, captivate

Antonyms: bore, ignore, distract, reject

English Example: Despite a fresh idea, Phillauri is a loosely-written film that fails to engross the audience.

Hindi Example: एक नए विचार के बावजूद, फिल्लौरी एक ढीली लिखित फिल्म है जो दर्शकों का ध्यान खींचने में नाकाम रही है।

 **Date: 2017/03/29**

WOD: *Emphatic*

Pronunciation: इम्फ़ेटिक

Type of word (Category): Adjective

English meaning: expressing something forcibly and clearly

Hindi meaning: ज़ोरदार

Synonyms: forceful, assertive, energetic, strong, certain, direct

Antonyms: insignificant, unassertive, forceless, subtle

English Example: India ended the home season with an emphatic way by winning the Border-Gavaskar Trophy.

Hindi Example: भारत ने बॉर्डर-गावस्कर ट्रॉफी जीतकर घरेलू सीजन को एक ज़ोरदार तरीके से समाप्त किया।

Date: 2017/03/30

WOD: *Tarnish*

Pronunciation: टा-र्निश

Type of word (Category): Verb

English meaning: make or become less valuable or respected

Hindi meaning: कलंकित करना

Synonyms: sully, besmirch, taint, spoil, ruin, disgrace, defame, undermine

Antonyms: purify, clean, dignify, glorify

English Example: Clarke slammed Aussie media for tarnishing Kohli's image.

Hindi Example: क्लार्क ने कोहली की छवि कलंकित करने के लिए ऑस्ट्रेलियाई मीडिया की आलोचना की।

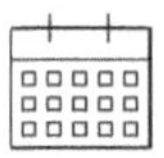

WOD: *Assent*

Pronunciation: अ-सेन्ट

Type of word (Category): Verb

English meaning: express approval or agreement

Hindi meaning: स्वीकृति देना

Synonyms: accept, approve, consent, sanction, allow, authorize

Antonyms: dissent, disagree, reject, disapprove, deny

English Example: President Pranab Mukherjee has given assent to the Maternity Benefit (Amendment) Act, 2017.

Hindi Example: राष्ट्रपति प्रणब मुखर्जी ने मातृत्व लाभ (संशोधन) अधिनियम, 2017 को स्वीकृति दी है।

April 2017

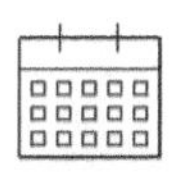 **Date: 2017/04/01**

WOD: *Kerfuffle*

Pronunciation: केर-फुफ्फल

Type of word (Category): Noun

English meaning: a commotion or fuss, especially one caused by conflicting views, a disorderly outburst or tumult

Hindi meaning: शोर शराबा

Synonyms: commotion, disturbance, fuss, turmoil, stir

Antonyms: order, calm, arrangement, peacefulness

English Example: A Twitter post on MS Dhoni's Adhaar application by an excited enrolment centre official led to an online kerfuffle.

Hindi Example: एक उत्साहित नामांकन केंद्र के अधिकारी द्वारा एमएस धोनी के आधार आवेदन पर एक ट्विटर पोस्ट ने ऑनलाइन शोर शराबे को आगे बढ़ाया।

Date: 2017/04/02

WOD: *Sturdy*

Pronunciation: स्टर्डी

Type of word (Category): Adjective

English meaning: (of a person or their body) strongly and solidly built

Hindi meaning: मज़बूत

Synonyms: well built, strong, tough, firm, powerful, robust

Antonyms: fragile, delicate, weak, unstable

English Example: Taapsee is a sturdy modern Indian girl and she plays it in her film 'Naam Shabana'.

Hindi Example: तापसी एक मज़बूत आधुनिक भारतीय लड़की है और वह इसे अपनी फिल्म 'नाम शबाना' में निभाती है।

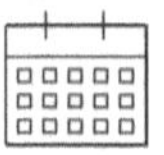

Date: 2017/04/03

WOD: *Stunning*

Pronunciation: स्टनिंग

Type of word (Category): Adjective

English meaning: extremely impressive or attractive

Hindi meaning: शानदार

Synonyms: remarkable, extraordinary, incredible, impressive, outstanding, amazing, astonishing, marvellous

Antonyms: ugly, dreadful, unattractive, unimpressive

English Example: The first look of 'Half-Girlfriend', based on Chetan Bhagat's novel, is looking stunning.

Hindi Example: चेतन भगत के उपन्यास पर आधारित 'हाफ-गर्लफ्रेंड'; का पहला रूप, शानदार लग रहा है।

Date: 2017/04/04

WOD: *Avenge*

Pronunciation: अ-वेन्ज

Type of word (Category): Verb

English meaning: inflict harm in return for (an injury or wrong done to oneself or another)

Hindi meaning: बदला लेना

Synonyms: revenge, retaliate, punish, vindicate, repay

Antonyms: forgive, dismiss, absolve, apologize

English Example: Dominant P.V. Sindhu avenged Rio Olympic loss by beating Carolina Marin in India Open Super Series.

Hindi Example: प्रभावी पी.वी. सिंधु ने भारत ओपन सुपर सीरीज में कैरोलिना मारिन को हराकर रियो ओलंपिक हार का बदला लिया।

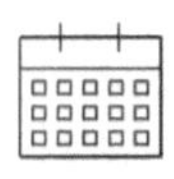 **Date: 2017/04/05**

WOD: *Strive*

Pronunciation: स्ट्रा-इव

Type of word (Category): *Verb*

English meaning: *make great efforts to achieve or obtain something, struggle or fight vigorously*

Hindi meaning: संघर्ष करना

Synonyms: *struggle, contend, attempt, try, fight, endeavour*

Antonyms: *relax, forget, skip, break*

English Example: *Sakshi Malik was born in a normal middle-class family and strove to excel in sports.*

Hindi Example: साक्षी मलिक एक सामान्य मध्यवर्गीय परिवार में पैदा हुई और खेल में उत्कृष्टता हासिल करने के लिए संघर्ष किया।

Date: 2017/04/06

WOD: *Creepy*

Pronunciation: क्रीपी

Type of word (Category): *Adjective*

English meaning: *causing an unpleasant feeling of fear or unease*

Hindi meaning: खौफनाक

Synonyms: *terrifying, frightening, dreadful, scary, sinister, ghostly*

Antonyms: *pleasant, peaceful, calming, pleasing*

English Example: *'The Mummy' new trailer shows more of Sofia Boutella's creepy villain.*

Hindi Example: 'द ममी' का नया ट्रेलर सोफिया ब्यूटेले को अधिक ख़ौफनाक खलनायक दिखाता है।

Date: 2017/04/07

WOD: *Vie*

Pronunciation: वाइ

Type of word (Category):   *Verb*

English meaning: compete eagerly with someone in order to do or achieve something

Hindi meaning: प्रतिस्पर्धा करना

Synonyms: compete, contend, contest, struggle, fight, battle

Antonyms: aid, assist, help, support

English Example: Over the next 46 days, the eight teams of the Indian Premier League will vie for the top position.

Hindi Example: अगले 46 दिनों तक, इंडियन प्रीमियर लीग की आठ टीमें सर्वोच्च पद के लिए प्रतिस्पर्धा करेंगी।

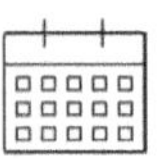

Date:2017/04/08

WOD: *Refute*

Pronunciation: रि-फ़्यूट

Type of word (Category):   *Verb*

English meaning: prove (a statement or theory) to be wrong or false

Hindi meaning: खण्डन करना

Synonyms: disprove, contradict, deny, oppose, invalidate, rebut

Antonyms: prove, confirm, agree, certify

English Example: Sunil Grover refuted reports of being offered any new show.

Hindi Example: सुनील ग्रोवर ने किसी भी नए शो की पेशकश की रिपोर्ट का खण्डन किया।

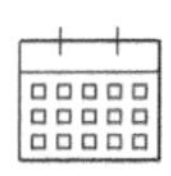 **Date: 2017/04/09**

WOD: *Outcry*

Pronunciation: आउट्क्राइ

Type of word (Category): Noun

English meaning: a strong expression of anger and disapproval about something, made by a group of people or by the public

Hindi meaning: कड़ा विरोध

Synonyms: indignation, fuss, commotion, uproar, row, outbursts, tumult, opposition

Antonyms: silence, peace, acknowledgment, acceptance

English Example: Pepsi pulled controversial Kendall Jenner ad after outcry.

Hindi Example: पेप्सी ने कड़े विरोध के बाद विवादास्पद केंडल जेनर का विज्ञापन रोका।

Date: 2017/04/10

WOD: *Half Girlfriend*

Pronunciation: हाफ़ गॅःलफ्रेंड

Type of word (Category): Noun

English meaning: more than a friend but less than a lover (girlfriend)

Hindi meaning: दोस्त से ज्यादा और गर्लफ्रेंड से कम

Synonyms: close friend

Antonyms: -

English Example: Riya did not want to be Madhav's girlfriend, but she proposed to be his half girlfriend.

Hindi Example: रिया माधव की प्रेमिका नहीं बनना चाहती थी, लेकिन उसने उसकी दोस्त से ज्यादा और गर्लफ्रेंड से कम होने का प्रस्ताव रखा।

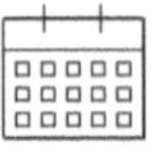 **Date: 2017/04/11**

WOD: *Promising*

Pronunciation: प्रामि-सिंग

Type of word (Category):   *Adjective*

English meaning: *showing signs of future success*

Hindi meaning: आशाजनक

Synonyms: *good, encouraging, favourable, hopeful, full of promise, optimistic, positive, reassuring*

Antonyms: *hopeless, unfavourable, inauspicious, gloomy*

English Example: *The trailer of Half Girlfriend is looking promising.*

Hindi Example: हॉफ गर्लफ्रेंड का ट्रेलर आशाजनक दिख रहा है।

Date: 2017/04/12

WOD: *Demeanour*

Pronunciation: डि-मी-अ

Type of word (Category):   *Noun*

English meaning: *outward behaviour or bearing, behavior toward others*

Hindi meaning: आचरण

Synonyms: *behavior, conduct, bearing, manner, attitude*

Antonyms: -

English Example: *Harbhajan Singh disclosed his childhood demeanour in 'Taste Match' TV show.*

Hindi Example: हरभजन सिंह ने अपने बचपन के आचरण के बारे में 'टेस्ट मैच' टीवी शो में खुलासा किया।

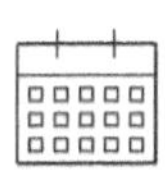 **Date: 2017/04/13**

WOD: *Breathtaking*

Pronunciation: ब्रेथ-टेकिंग

Type of word (Category): Adjective

English meaning: astonishing or awe-inspiring in quality, so as to take one's breath away

Hindi meaning: असाधारण

Synonyms: spectacular, wonderful, awesome, astonishing, amazing, stunning, stupendous, incredible

Antonyms: boring, dull, tedious, disgusting

English Example: Half Girlfriend's breathtaking 'Baarish' song will instantly connect viewers with the romance.

Hindi Example: हॉफ गर्लफ्रेंड का असाधारण 'बारिश' गीत दर्शकों को तुरंत प्रेम कथा के साथ जोड़ देगा।

Date: 2017/04/14

WOD: *Workaholic*

Pronunciation: वर्कहा-लिक

Type of word (Category): Noun

English meaning: a person who compulsively works excessively hard and long hours

Hindi meaning: अत्यधिक काम करने वाला

Synonyms: overachiever, work addict, very hard worker, workhorse, worker

Antonyms: idler, lazy

English Example: PM Narendra Modi is known to be an extremely workaholic person among his peers and critics.

Hindi Example: प्रधान मंत्री नरेंद्र मोदी अपने साथियों और समीक्षकों के बीच अत्यधिक काम करने वाले व्यक्ति माने जाते हैं।

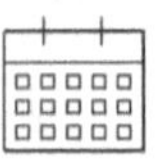

Date: 2017/04/15

WOD: *Roast*

Pronunciation: रोस्ट

Type of word (Category): *Verb*

English meaning: *criticize or reprimand severely*

Hindi meaning: तीव्र आलोचना करना

Synonyms: *lambaste, lampoon, ridicule*

Antonyms: *praise*

English Example: *Actor Abhay Deol roasted fellow actors on Facebook for endorsing fairness creams.*

Hindi Example: अभिनेता अभय देओल ने फेसबुक पर साथी कलाकारों की सुंदरता क्रीम के लिए विज्ञापन करने की तीव्र आलोचना की।

Date: 2017/04/16

WOD: *Poignantly*

Pronunciation: पॉइन्यन्ट्ली

Type of word (Category): *Adverb*

English meaning: *in a way that evokes a keen sense of sadness or regret*

Hindi meaning: मर्मस्पर्शी ढंग से

Synonyms: *touchingly, affectingly, keenly, emotionally*

Antonyms: *cheerfully, unemotionally, apathetically, blankly*

English Example: *Aazaadiyan' song from Begum Jaan poignantly conveys the pain of partition.*

Hindi Example: बेगम जान का 'आजादीय' गीत मर्मस्पर्शी ढंग से विभाजन के दर्द को बताता है।

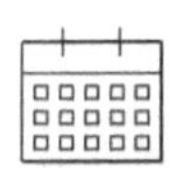 **Date: 2017/04/17**

WOD: *Deceased*

Pronunciation: डि-सीस्ट

Type of word (Category): Adjective

English meaning: recently dead

Hindi meaning: दिवंगत

Synonyms: dead, expired, departed, lifeless, demised

Antonyms: alive, active, awake, breathing

English Example: Akshay Kumar launched a new website 'Bharat Ke Veer' for the families of the deceased Indian soldiers.

Hindi Example: अक्षय कुमार ने दिवंगत भारतीय सैनिकों के परिवारों के लिए एक नई वेबसाइट 'भारत के वीर' का शुभारंभ किया।

Date: 2017/04/18

WOD: *Camaraderie*

Pronunciation: कैमॅ-रा-डॅरि

Type of word (Category): Noun

English meaning: mutual trust and friendship among people who spend a lot of time together

Hindi meaning: सौहार्द

Synonyms: friendship, fellowship, companionship, brotherliness, closeness, affinity, togetherness, comradeship

Antonyms: loneliness, enmity, animosity, disagreement

English Example: Ranveer Singh and Arjun Kapoor's off-screen camaraderie never failed to catch attention.

Hindi Example: रणवीर सिंह और अर्जुन कपूर की परदे के पीछे का सौहार्द ध्यान आकर्षित करने में कभी नाकाम नहीं रहा।

Date: 2017/04/19

WOD: *Croon*

Pronunciation: क्रून

Type of word (Category): Verb

English meaning: hum or sing in a soft, low voice, especially in a sentimental manner

Hindi meaning: गुनगुनाना

Synonyms: sing, hum, vocalize, carol, chorus

Antonyms: -

English Example: Crooned by Arijit Singh and Shashaa Tirupati 'Phir Bhi Tumko Chaahunga' song is worth to listen.

Hindi Example: अरिजीत सिंह और शाषा तिरुपति द्वारा गुनगुनाया गीत 'फिर भी तुमको चाहूंगा' सुनने लायक है।

Date: 2017/04/20

WOD: *Abscond*

Pronunciation: अब्स्कॉन्ड

Type of word (Category): Verb

English meaning: leave hurriedly and secretly, typically to escape from custody or avoid arrest

Hindi meaning: फ़रार हो जाना

Synonyms: flee, decamp, escape, run away, fly, disappear

Antonyms: remain, stay, appear, stop

English Example: Absconding liquor baron Vijay Mallya was arrested and released on bail in London on Tuesday.

Hindi Example: फरार हो गए शराब व्यापारी विजय माल्या को लंदन में मंगलवार को गिरफ्तार कर जमानत पर रिहा कर दिया गया।

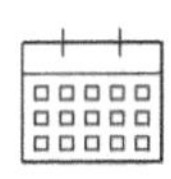 **Date: 2017/04/21**

WOD: *Swashbuckling*

Pronunciation: स्वॉश्बर्क्लिंग

Type of word (Category): Adjective

English meaning: behaving in a brave and exciting way, especially like a fighter in the past

Hindi meaning: साहसिक

Synonyms: adventurous, dashing, daring, daredevil, bold

Antonyms: unadventurous

English Example: Swashbuckling West Indian batsman Chris Gayle became the first cricketer to score 10,000 runs in T20 cricket.

Hindi Example: वेस्ट इंडीज के साहसिक बल्लेबाज क्रिस गेल टी 20 क्रिकेट में 10,000 रन बनाने वाले पहले क्रिकेटर बन गए।

Date: 2017/04/22

WOD: *Stun*

Pronunciation: स्टन

Type of word (Category): Verb

English meaning: astonish or shock (someone) so that they are temporarily unable to react

Hindi meaning: अत्यधिक प्रभावित कर देना

Synonyms: astonish, amaze, stupefy, astound, startle, shock

Antonyms: bore, surrender

English Example: Shraddha Kapoor stuns everyone as a basketball player in Half Girlfriend poster.

Hindi Example: हॉफ गर्लफ्रेंड के पोस्टर में एक बास्केटबॉल खिलाड़ी के रूप में श्रद्धा कपूर सभी को अत्यधिक प्रभावित कर देती है।

WOD: *Congregate*

Pronunciation: कॉन्ग्रि-गेट

Type of word (Category): *Verb*

English meaning: *gather into a crowd or mass*

Hindi meaning: एकत्र होना

Synonyms: *gather, assemble, collect, meet, convene, crowd*

Antonyms: *separate, scatter, divide, disperse*

English Example: *Dressed as Charlie Chaplin, a crowd congregated at his home to celebrate his 128th birthday.*

Hindi Example: चार्ली चैपलिन की तरह कपड़े पहनकर, भीड़ उनके घर पर उनका 128वां जन्मदिन मनाने एकत्र हुई।

WOD: *Queasy*

Pronunciation: क्वीज़ी

Type of word (Category): *Adjective*

English meaning: *feeling sick, slightly nervous or worried about something*

Hindi meaning: व्याकुल

Synonyms: *uneasy, nauseous, sick, anxious, nervous*

Antonyms: *healthy, comfortable, untroubled, satisfied*

English Example: *Raveena Tandon's comeback movie Maatr is relevant but makes you queasy.*

Hindi Example: रवीना टंडन की वापसी फिल्म मातृ प्रासंगिक है, लेकिन आपको व्याकुल करती है।

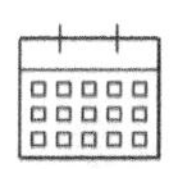

Date: 2017/04/25

WOD: *Abject*

Pronunciation: ऐब्जेक्ट

Type of word (Category): Adjective

English meaning: (of a situation or condition) extremely unpleasant and degrading

Hindi meaning: दयनीय

Synonyms: wretched, miserable, hopeless, pathetic, woeful, lamentable, degrading, appalling

Antonyms: worthy, noble, commendable, magnificent

English Example: Virat Kohli let down by RCB's abject batting display.

Hindi Example: विराट कोहली को आरसीबी की दयनीय बल्लेबाजी प्रदर्शन ने निराश किया।

Date: 2017/04/26

WOD: *Lingo*

Pronunciation: लिं-गो

Type of word (Category): Noun

English meaning: The vocabulary or jargon of a particular subject or group of people

Hindi meaning: शब्दावली

Synonyms: jargon, argot, language, slang, dialect, vocabulary

Antonyms: standard, quiet

English Example: The trailer of 'Hanuman Da Damdaar' uses a modern lingo to attract Indian kids.

Hindi Example: हनुमान दा दमदार' का ट्रेलर भारतीय बच्चों को आकर्षित करने के लिए आधुनिक शब्दावली का प्रयोग करता है।

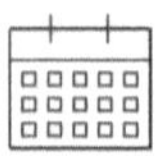 **Date: 2017/04/27**

WOD: *Mesmerising*

Pronunciation: मेज़्म-रा-इज़िंग

Type of word (Category):   Adjective

English meaning: So attractive or interesting that you do not notice or pay attention to anything else around you

Hindi meaning: मंत्रमुग्ध कर देने वाला

Synonyms: hypnotic, fascinating, spellbinding, enchanting, captivating, charming

Antonyms: boring, flat, dull, monotonous

English Example: 'Thodi Der' is a mesmerising track from Half Girlfriend that will touch your heart for sure.

Hindi Example: 'थोड़ी देर' हाफ गर्लफ्रेंड का मंत्रमुग्ध कर देने वाला ट्रैक है जो निश्चित रूप से आपके दिल को छू लेगा।

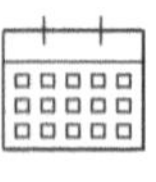 **Date: 2017/04/28**

WOD: *Initiative*

Pronunciation: इनि-श-टिव

Type of word (Category):   Noun

English meaning: The power or opportunity to act or take charge before others do

Hindi meaning: पहल

Synonyms: opening move, introductory, inaugural, incipient, leadership

Antonyms: lethargy, closing, apathy, laziness

English Example: Bill Gates lauded PM Narendra Modi for 'success' of Swachh Bharat initiative.

Hindi Example: बिल गेट्स ने प्रधान मंत्री नरेंद्र मोदी की स्वच्छ भारत पहल की 'सफलता' के लिए सराहना की।

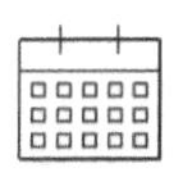

Date: 2017/04/29

WOD: *Drench*

Pronunciation: ड्रेन्च

Type of word (Category):   *Verb*

English meaning: *wet thoroughly, soak*

Hindi meaning: सराबोर करना

Synonyms: *soak, immerse, douse, wet thoroughly, drown, submerge*
dry

Antonyms: *dry, dehydrate, parch*

English Example: *Baahubali 2: The Conclusion is drenched in emotions with grand spectacle.*

Hindi Example: बाहुबली 2: द कन्क्लूज़न भव्य प्रदर्शन के साथ भावनाओं से सराबोर है।

Date: 2017/04/30

WOD: *Perennial*

Pronunciation: प-रेनीअल

Type of word (Category):   *Adjective*

English meaning: *lasting or existing for a long or apparently infinite time, enduring or continually recurring*

Hindi meaning: सदाबहार

Synonyms: *everlasting, eternal, endless, permanent, constant, perpetual*

Antonyms: *short, brief*

English Example: *Zeenat Aman paid a touching tribute to Vinod Khanna, called him a perennial handsome actor.*

Hindi Example: ज़ीनत अमान ने विनोद खन्ना को मर्मस्पर्शी श्रद्धांजलि अर्पित की, उन्हें एक सदाबहार ख़ूबसूरत अभिनेता कहा।

HinKhoj

20 Million + Download

World Largest English Hindi Dictionary

- Offline mode
- Word of the Day
- Learning Game
- Synonyms, Antonyms and Sentence example

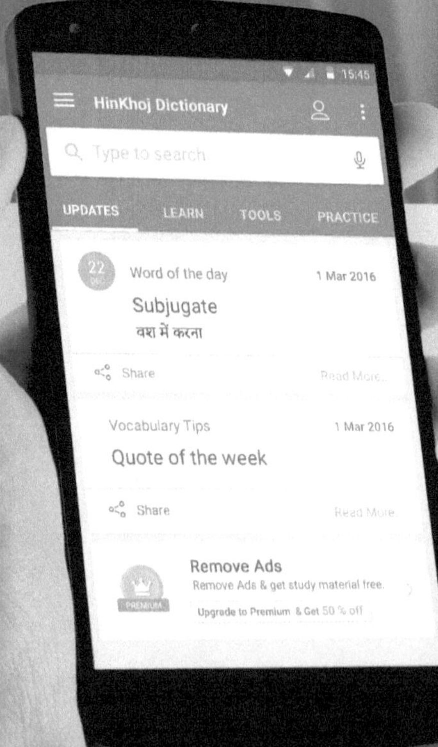

Give a missed call & Downlo
90157-10033

Scan QR code
to download the App

May 2017

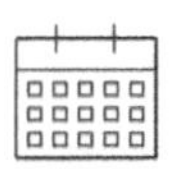 **Date: 2017/05/01**

WOD: *Ambush*

Pronunciation: ऐम्बुश

Type of word (Category): Noun

English meaning: a surprise attack by people lying in wait in a concealed position

Hindi meaning: घात

Synonyms: trap, attack, ambuscade, trick, pitfall

Antonyms: retreat, completion, closure

English Example: KKR on field saluted to the CRPF soldiers who lost their lives in Sukma ambush.

Hindi Example: मैदान पर कोलकाता नाइट राइडर्स ने सीआरपीएफ सैनिक को सलामी दी जो सुकमा घात में अपनी जान गंवा चुके हैं।

Date: 2017/05/02

WOD: *Contention*

Pronunciation: कॉन्टेन्शॅन

Type of word (Category): Noun

English meaning: a striving in rivalry, competition or contest

Hindi meaning: प्रतिस्पर्धा

Synonyms: clash, competition, conflict, combat

Antonyms: agreement, peace, serenity

English Example: RCB became first team to be thrown out of contention for IPL playoffs.

Hindi Example: आरसीबी आईपीएल प्लेऑफ़ की प्रतिस्पर्धा से बाहर हो जाने वाली पहली टीम बन गई।

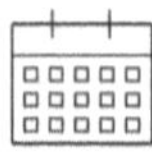

Date: 2017/05/03

WOD: *Tout*

Pronunciation: टाउट

Type of word (Category): *Verb*

English meaning: to advertise, talk about, or praise something or someone repeatedly, especially as a way of encouraging people to like, accept, or buy something

Hindi meaning: प्रस्तुत करना

Synonyms: promote, proclaim, publicize, acclaim, boost

Antonyms: conceal, hide, discourage

English Example: Sarabhai Vs Sarabhai Take 2 is touted as a blend of clean, crazy comedy.

Hindi Example: साराभाई बनाम साराभाई टेक 2 को एक साफ, अत्यंत उत्साहपूर्ण कॉमेडी के एक मिश्रण के रूप में प्रस्तुत किया गया है।

Date: 2017/05/04

WOD: *Groovy*

Pronunciation: ग्रूवी

Type of word (Category): Adjective

English meaning: fashionable and exciting, excellent

Hindi meaning: बढ़िया

Synonyms: great, wonderful, fabulous, fantastic, splendid, sensational

Antonyms: bad, poor, inferior, styleless

English Example: The super groovy song from Half Girlfriend 'mere dil mein' is released now.

Hindi Example: हाफ गर्लफ्रेंड का बहुत ही बढ़िया गीत 'मेरे दिल में' अब रिलीज हो गया है।

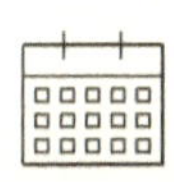 **Date: 2017/05/05**

WOD: *Beam*

Pronunciation: बीम

Type of word (Category): *Verb*

English meaning: *smile radiantly; express joy through one's facial expression*

Hindi meaning: मुस्कराना

Synonyms: *grin, smile, cheerful, happy, delighted, overjoyed*

Antonyms: *darken, frown, gloom*

English Example: *Anil Kapoor was beaming with joy and was clicking pictures as Sonam was honoured with the National award.*

Hindi Example: अनिल कपूर खुशी के साथ मुस्कुरा रहे थे और तस्वीरें क्लिक कर रहे थे जब सोनम को नेशनल पुरस्कार से सम्मानित किया गया था।

Date: 2017/05/06

WOD: *Obeisance*

Pronunciation: ओबे-सन्स

Type of word (Category): *Noun*

English meaning: *a gesture expressing deferential respect, such as a bow or curtsy*

Hindi meaning: अभिवादन

Synonyms: *respect, homage, worship, adoration, reverence, respectfulness, honour, submission*

Antonyms: *disobedience, disrespect, dishonor, disregard*

English Example: *PM Narendra Modi paid obeisance at Kedarnath temple on Wednesday.*

Hindi Example: प्रधान मंत्री नरेंद्र मोदी ने बुधवार को केदारनाथ मंदिर में अभिवादन किया।

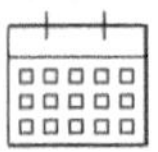 **Date: 2017/05/07**

WOD: *Comedienne*

Pronunciation: कमी-डीइन

Type of word (Category):   *Noun*

English meaning: *a female comedian*

Hindi meaning: हास्य अभिनेत्री

Synonyms: *comedian, humorist, clown, entertainer*

Antonyms: -

English Example: *The Kapil Sharma Show's comedienne Sugandha Mishra rubbished marriage rumour.*

Hindi Example: कपिल शर्मा शो की हास्य अभिनेत्री सुगंधा मिश्रा ने शादी की अफवाह को खारिज कर दिया।

 Date: 2017/05/08

WOD: *Unearth*

Pronunciation: अ-नर्थ

Type of word (Category):   *Verb*

English meaning: *find (something) in the ground by digging*

Hindi meaning: खोद निकालना

Synonyms: *disentomb, unbury, excavate, discovered, exhumed*

Antonyms: *buried, put back, submerged*

English Example: *Scientists have unearthed 70 million-year-old five ancient dinosaur egg fossils in China.*

Hindi Example: वैज्ञानिकों ने चीन में 70 मिलियन साल पुराने पांच प्राचीन डायनासोर अंडे के जीवाश्मों को खोद निकाला है।

MAY

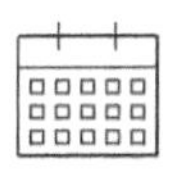

Date: 2017/05/09

WOD: *Decimate*

Pronunciation: डेसिमेट

Type of word (Category): *Verb*

English meaning: kill, destroy, or remove a large proportion of, to cause great destruction or harm to

Hindi meaning: बरबाद करना

Synonyms: destroy, wipe out, crush, devastate, ruin, smash

Antonyms: construct, fix, revamp, create

English Example: Sunil Narine's fastest fifty in IPL 10 decimated RCB completely.

Hindi Example: आईपीएल 10 में सुनील नारायण के सबसे तेज अर्धशतक ने आरसीबी को पूरी तरह से बरबाद कर दिया।

Date: 2017/05/10

WOD: *Rave*

Pronunciation: रेव

Type of word (Category): *Verb*

English meaning: speak or write about someone or something with great enthusiasm or admiration

Hindi meaning: अत्यधिक प्रशंसा करना

Synonyms: praise, applaud, laud, acclaim, cheer

Antonyms: criticize, condemn, discourage, denounce

English Example: Fans are raving for the Justin Bieber concert in India.

Hindi Example: भारत में जस्टिन बीबर कॉन्सर्ट के लिए प्रशंसक अत्यधिक प्रशंसा कर रहे हैं।

WOD: *Goofy*

Pronunciation: गूफी

Type of word (Category): *Adjective*

English meaning: *being crazy, ridiculous, or mildly ludicrous especially in a funny or pleasant way*

Hindi meaning: हास्यास्पद

Synonyms: *silly, ridiculous, crazy, funny, nutty*

Antonyms: *smart, sane, sensible, serious*

English Example: *Katrina Kaif shared her pictures in a goofy pose on Instagram.*

Hindi Example: कैटरीना कैफ ने इंस्टाग्राम पर हास्यास्पद मुद्रा में अपनी तस्वीरों को साझा किया।

WOD: *Farrago*

Pronunciation: फरागो

Type of word (Category): *Noun*

English meaning: *a confused mixture*

Hindi meaning: गड़बड़झाला

Synonyms: *mess, confusion, hotchpotch, mixture, jumble, confusion, olio, disarray*

Antonyms: *organize, structure*

English Example: *Shashi Tharoor considered the allegations regarding Sunanda's death a farrago of distortions and misrepresentations.*

Hindi Example: शशि थरूर ने सुनंदा की मौत के बारे में आरोपों को विकृतियों और गलत प्रस्तुतिकरण का गड़बड़झाला माना।

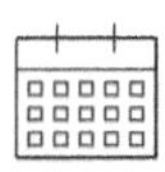 **Date: 2017/05/13**

WOD: *Emote*

Pronunciation: इ-मोट

Type of word (Category): *Verb*

English meaning: *to show emotion in a way that makes it very clear what you are feeling*

Hindi meaning: भावना व्यक्त करना

Synonyms: *act, perform, dramatize, represent, overact, play*

Antonyms: *play down*

English Example: *Shraddha Kapoor is able to emote herself perfectly in the new song 'Phir Bhi Tumko Chaahungi'.*

Hindi Example: श्रद्धा कपूर पूरी तरह से नए गीत 'फिर भी तुमको चाहुंगी' में अपनी भावना व्यक्त करने में सक्षम है।

Date: 2017/05/14

WOD: *Devise*

Pronunciation: डि-वाइज़

Type of word (Category): *Verb*

English meaning: *to invent a plan, system, object, etc., usually using your intelligence or imagination*

Hindi meaning: आविष्कार करना

Synonyms: *contrive, create, invent, concoct, originate, conceive, produce, develop*

Antonyms: *disorganized, copy, borrow, duplicate*

English Example: *PM Modi devised a new formula – Information technology plus Indian talent is equal to India tomorrow.*

Hindi Example: प्रधानमंत्री मोदी ने एक नए सूत्र का आविष्कार किया – सूचना प्रौद्योगिकी और भारतीय प्रतिभा भारत के भविष्य के बराबर है।

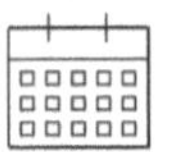 **Date: 2017/05/15**

WOD: *Incredibly*

Pronunciation: इन्क्रे-डब्ली

Type of word (Category): *Adverb*

English meaning: *used for saying that something is very difficult to believe, to a great degree; extremely*

Hindi meaning: अविश्वसनीय रूप से

Synonyms: *unbelievably, amazingly, astonishingly, extraordinarily, inconceivably*

Antonyms: *believably, credibly, probably, hardly*

English Example: *Kapil Dev unveiled his incredibly detailed wax statue at Madame Tussauds museum in New Delhi.*

Hindi Example: कपिल देव ने नई दिल्ली में मैडम तुसाद संग्रहालय में अपनी अविश्वसनीय रूप से विस्तृत मोम प्रतिमा का अनावरण किया।

 **Date: 2017/05/16**

WOD: *Veteran*

Pronunciation: वे-टरन

Type of word (Category): *Noun*

English meaning: *a person who has had long experience in a particular field*

Hindi meaning: अनुभवी

Synonyms: *experienced, expert, professional, master, proficient*

Antonyms: *amateur, learner, novice, beginner*

English Example: *Veteran batsman Yuvraj Singh is hopeful to make his 'meaningful' contribution in Champions Trophy.*

Hindi Example: अनुभवी बल्लेबाज युवराज सिंह को उम्मीद है कि चैंपियंस ट्रॉफी में उनका 'सार्थक' योगदान होगा।

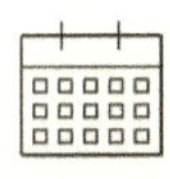 **Date: 2017/05/17**

WOD: *Mammoth*

Pronunciation: मेमथ

Type of word (Category):   Adjective

English meaning: extremely large

Hindi meaning: विशाल

Synonyms: huge, enormous, gigantic, giant, colossal, massive, vast, immense, mighty

Antonyms: tiny, small, little

English Example: Indian women's cricket team made a mammoth 358 runs against Ireland.

Hindi Example: भारतीय महिला क्रिकेट टीम ने आयरलैंड के खिलाफ विशाल 358 रन बनाए।

Date: 2017/05/18

WOD: *Scramble*

Pronunciation: स्क्रैम्बॅल

Type of word (Category):   Verb

English meaning: an unceremonious and disorganized struggle, Struggle or compete with others for something in an eager or uncontrolled and undignified way

Hindi meaning: संघर्ष करना

Synonyms: struggle, scuffle, jostle, tussle, battle, compete, contend, vie

Antonyms: unscramble, retreat, stop, rest

English Example: Security officials around the world are scrambling to find who was behind 'ransomware' cyberattack.

Hindi Example: दुनिया भर के सुरक्षा अधिकारी यह पता लगाने के लिए संघर्ष कर रहे हैं कि 'रेन्समवेयर' साइबरअटैक के पीछे कौन था।

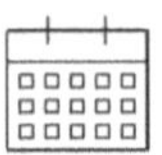 **Date: 2017/05/19**

WOD: *Anticipated*

Pronunciation: ऐन्टिस-पेटड

Type of word (Category):   *Adjective*

English meaning: *expected hopefully*

Hindi meaning: अपेक्षित

Synonyms: *expected, awaited, forthcoming, promising, likely, foreseen*

Antonyms: *unexpected, sudden, unanticipated*

English Example: *The most anticipated movie 'Half Girlfriend' is released today.*

Hindi Example: सबसे अधिक अपेक्षित फिल्म 'हॉफ गर्लफ्रेंड' आज रिलीज हुई है।

Date: 2017/05/20

WOD: *Confiscate*

Pronunciation: कान्फिस्केट

Type of word (Category):   *Verb*

English meaning: *take or seize (someone's property) with authority*

Hindi meaning: ज़ब्त करना

Synonyms: *impound, seize, commandeer, requisition, appropriate, expropriate, take possession of*

Antonyms: *give, offer, provide*

English Example: *Vijay Mallya's Rs. 100-crore 'Beach Villa' was confiscated by ED.*

Hindi Example: विजय मात्या के 100 करोड़ रुपये का 'बीच विला' को ईडी द्वारा जब्त कर लिया गया।

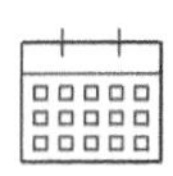 **Date: 2017/05/21**

WOD: *Exempt*

Pronunciation: इग्ज़ेम्प्ट

Type of word (Category):   *Verb*

English meaning: *free (a person or organization) from an obligation or liability imposed on others*

Hindi meaning: मुक्त करना

Synonyms: *free, excuse, absolve, relieve, exclude*

Antonyms: *apply, enforce, implement*

English Example: *GST Council on Friday exempted healthcare and education from the tax.*

Hindi Example: जीएसटी परिषद ने शुक्रवार को स्वास्थ्य सेवा और शिक्षा को टैक्स से मुक्त कर दिया।

Date: 2017/05/22

WOD: *Void*

Pronunciation: वॉइड

Type of word (Category):   *Noun*

English meaning: *a completely empty space*

Hindi meaning: खाली जगह

Synonyms: *gap, empty space, blank, vacuum, emptiness, abyss*

Antonyms: *fullness, fill*

English Example: *Many in Tamil Nadu feel that only Rajinikanth can fill the void left by Jayalalithaa in politics.*

Hindi Example: तमिलनाडु में कई लोगों का मानना है कि राजनीति में जयललिता के द्वारा छोड़ी गई खाली जगह केवल रजनीकांत भर सकते है।

📅 **Date: 2017/05/23**

WOD: *Entice*

Pronunciation: इन्टाइस

Type of word (Category):   *Verb*

English meaning: *attract or tempt by offering pleasure or advantage*

Hindi meaning: लुभाना

Synonyms: *tempt, allure, lure, attract, inveigle, invite*

Antonyms: *repel, dissuade, deter, repulse*

English Example: *Arjun Kapoor and Shraddha Kapoor's Half Girlfriend has managed to entice the audience during the weekend.*

Hindi Example: अर्जुन कपूर और श्रद्धा कपूर की हॉफ गर्लफ्रेंड सप्ताहांत के दौरान दर्शकों को लुभाने में सफ़ल रही है।

📅 **Date: 2017/05/24**

WOD: *Unison*

Pronunciation: यूनि-सन

Type of word (Category):   *Noun*

English meaning: *acting or speaking together, or at the same time*

Hindi meaning: एक सुर

Synonyms: *harmony, unity, agreement, concurrence, accordance, concord*

Antonyms: *disharmony, disagreement, chaos, discord, conflict*

English Example: *The cricket fraternity praised the Rohit Sharma-led Mumbai Indians in unison after IPL final.*

Hindi Example: आईपीएल फाइनल के बाद रोहित शर्मा की अगुवाई वाली मुंबई इंडियंस की क्रिकेट बिरादरी ने एक सुर में तारीफ की।

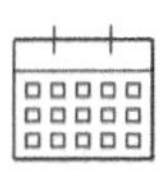
Date: 2017/05/25

WOD: *Mayhem*

Pronunciation: मेहेम

Type of word (Category): Noun

English meaning: a situation in which there is little or no order or control, violent or extreme disorder

Hindi meaning: अफरा तफरी

Synonyms: chaos, disorder, confusion, havoc, destruction, tumult, uproar, turmoil

Antonyms: calm, harmony, peace, discipline

English Example: Ariana Grande's concert in Manchester turned into mayhem after bomb blast.

Hindi Example: मैनचेस्टर में एरियाना ग्रांडे का कॉन्सर्ट बम विस्फोट के बाद अफरा-तफरी में बदल गया।

Date: 2017/05/26

WOD: *Bigwig*

Pronunciation: बिग्विग

Type of word (Category): Noun

English meaning: an important person, especially in a particular sphere

Hindi meaning: अहम शख़्स

Synonyms: notable, celebrity, dignitary, personage, VIP, important person

Antonyms: nobody, nonentity, cipher

English Example: Many Bollywood bigwigs along with Indian cricket team attended the premiere of Sachin: A Billion Dreams.

Hindi Example: भारतीय क्रिकेट टीम के साथ बॉलीवुड के कई अहम शख़्सों ने सचिन: ए बिलियन ड्रीम्स के प्रीमियर में भाग लिया।

WOD: *Spooky*

Pronunciation: स्पूकी

Type of word (Category): Adjective

English meaning: sinister or ghostly in a way that causes fear and unease

Hindi meaning: डरावना

Synonyms: eerie, sinister, ghostly, uncanny, weird, unearthly, mysterious, frightening, scary

Antonyms: ordinary, natural, unfrightening, earthly, natural

English Example: Jayalalithaa's Poes Garden residence has turned into one of the spookiest places in Chennai.

Hindi Example: जयललिता का पोज गार्डन निवास चेन्नई में सबसे डरावनी जगहों में से एक बन गया है।

WOD: *Withstand*

Pronunciation: विथ्स्टेन्ड

Type of word (Category): Verb

English meaning: remain undamaged or unaffected by, resist

Hindi meaning: सहन करना

Synonyms: resist, endure, bear, suffer, tolerate

Antonyms: surrender, succumb, submit, comply

English Example: Dhola-Sadiya bridge over the Brahmaputra river is capable of withstanding the weight of a 60-tonne battle tank.

Hindi Example: ब्रह्मपुत्र नदी पर ढोला-सदिया पुल 60-टन युद्ध के टैंक का वजन सहन करने में सक्षम है।

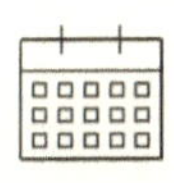
Date: 2017/05/29

WOD: *Barrage*

Pronunciation: ब-राश

Type of word (Category):   Noun

English meaning: an overwhelming number of questions, criticisms, or complaints delivered simultaneously or in rapid succession

Hindi meaning: झड़ी

Synonyms: deluge, shower, storm, onslaught, blaze, outpouring

Antonyms: -

English Example: Shatrughan Sinha welcomed Rajinikanth's intent to join politics in a barrage of tweets.

Hindi Example: शत्रुघ्न सिन्हा ने रजनीकांत के राजनीति में शामिल होने के इरादे का ट्रीट्स की झड़ी से स्वागत किया।

Date: 2017/05/30

WOD: *Outshine*

Pronunciation: आउ-चाइन

Type of word (Category):   Verb

English meaning: be much better than (someone) in a particular area

Hindi meaning: से श्रेष्ठ होना

Synonyms: surpass, overshadow, outclass, better, top, transcend

Antonyms: aid, be inferior, lose, fail

English Example: Girls outshone boys in the CBSE Class 12 results declared on Sunday.

Hindi Example: रविवार को घोषित हुई सीबीएसई कक्षा 12 के परिणामों में लड़कियाँ लड़कों से श्रेष्ठ हुईं।

 **Date: 2017/05/31**

WOD: *Ideologue*

Pronunciation: आइडीअलोग

Type of word (Category):   Noun

English meaning: an adherent of an ideology especially one who is uncompromising and dogmatic

Hindi meaning: विचारक

Synonyms: ideologist, proponent, advocator, exponent, advocate

Antonyms: dabbler, dilettante, defeatist, pessimist, cynic

English Example: PM Modi paid tribute to RSS ideologue Vinayak Damodar Savarkar on his 134th birth anniversary.

Hindi Example: प्रधान मंत्री मोदी ने आरएसएस के विचारक विनायक दामोदर सावरकर को 134वीं जयंती पर श्रद्धांजलि अर्पित की।

June 2017

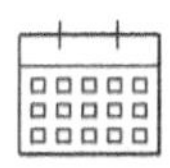 **Date: 2017/06/01**

WOD: *Nightmare*

Pronunciation: नाइट्मेर

Type of word (Category): Noun

English meaning: a very unpleasant or frightening experience or prospect

Hindi meaning: भयावह अनुभव

Synonyms: ordeal, horror, torment, trial, torture, burden, bane

Antonyms: pleasure, daymare, delight, wonderful, agreeable

English Example: Delhi University's unrealistic cut-offs is giving nightmares to students and parents.

Hindi Example: दिल्ली विश्वविद्यालय के अवास्तविक कट-ऑफ छात्रों और माता-पिता को भयावह अनुभव दे रहे है।

Date: 2017/06/02

WOD: *Respite*

Pronunciation: रेस-पाइट

Type of word (Category): Noun

English meaning: a short period of rest or relief from something difficult or unpleasant

Hindi meaning: आराम

Synonyms: rest, break, intermission, stop, reprieve, hiatus, relief

Antonyms: continuation, outburst, increase, advance, beginning

English Example: Delhi-NCR experienced a brief respite from the scorching heat on Wednesday.

Hindi Example: दिल्ली-एनसीआर ने बुधवार को झुलसाने वाली गर्मी से थोड़े समय का आराम का अनुभव किया।

 **Date: 2017/06/03**

WOD: Rift

Pronunciation: रिफ्ट

Type of word (Category): Noun

English meaning: a serious break in friendly relations

Hindi meaning: अनबन

Synonyms: breach, division, split, quarrel, disagreement, row, conflict

Antonyms: connection, agreement, reunion, closure

English Example: After Virat Kohli-Anil Kumble 'rift', Virender Sehwag applied for India coach post.

Hindi Example: विराट कोहली-अनिल कुंबले के 'अनबन' के बाद, वीरेंद्र सहवाग ने भारतीय कोच पद के लिए आवेदन किया।

Date: 2017/06/04

WOD: Unflappable

Pronunciation: अन्फ्लेपबल

Type of word (Category): Adjective

English meaning: having or showing calmness in a crisis

Hindi meaning: शान्त

Synonyms: imperturbable, unexcitable, cool, calm, self-controlled, self-possessed, unmoved, cool-headed

Antonyms: nervous, upset, worried, anxious

English Example: Unflappable Ananya Vinay won 90th Scripps National Spelling Bee title on Thursday.

Hindi Example: शान्त अनन्या विनय ने गुरुवार को 90वीं स्क्रिप्स नेशनल स्पेलिंग बी खिताब जीता।

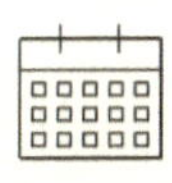 **Date: 2017/06/05**

WOD: *Aficionado*

Pronunciation: अफ़िश्य-नाडो

Type of word (Category): *Noun*

English meaning: *a person who is very knowledgeable and enthusiastic about an activity, subject, or pastime*

Hindi meaning: भक्त

Synonyms: *adorer, devotee, fan, addict, follower, admirer, adherent, fanatic*

Antonyms: *doubter, skeptic*

English Example: *A good news for chocolate aficionados, a new study has suggested that chocolate could be good for heart.*

Hindi Example: चॉकलेट भक्तों के लिए एक अच्छी खबर, एक नए अध्ययन ने सुझाव दिया है कि दिल के लिए चॉकलेट अच्छा होगा।

Date: 2017/06/06

WOD: *Resounding*

Pronunciation: री-साउन्डिंग

Type of word (Category): *Adjective*

English meaning: *marked by or uttered with forcefulness*

Hindi meaning: ज़बर्दस्त

Synonyms: *aggressive, assertive, dynamic, energetic, forceful, vigorous*

Antonyms: *guarded, mild, weak, nonassertive*

English Example: *India started their campaign with a resounding 124 run victory over Pakistan in Champions Trophy.*

Hindi Example: भारत ने पाकिस्तान पर 124 रनों की ज़बर्दस्त जीत के साथ चैंपियंस ट्रॉफी में अपना अभियान शुरू किया।

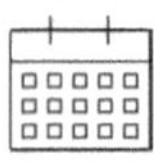

Date: 2017/06/07

WOD: *Searing*

Pronunciation: सिरिंग

Type of word (Category):   *Adjective*

English meaning: *extremely hot or intense*

Hindi meaning: बहुत तेज़

Synonyms: *scorching, blistering, burning, sizzling, broiling, sweltering, hot, fiery*

Antonyms: *cold, cool, freezing, chilly, frosty*

English Example: *Searing hot loo winds turned Delhi-NCR into a furnace.*

Hindi Example: बहुत तेज़ गर्म लू हवाओँ ने दिल्ली-एनसीआर को भट्टी में बदल दिया।

Date: 2017/06/08

WOD: *Persona*

Pronunciation: पर्सोना

Type of word (Category):   *Noun*

English meaning: *the aspect of someone's character that is presented to or perceived by others*

Hindi meaning: शख़्सियत

Synonyms: *image, face, personality, identity, guise, role*

Antonyms: -

English Example: *Salman Khan credits his onscreen persona to people working for him.*

Hindi Example: सलमान खान अपने परदे की शख़्सियत का श्रेय उनके लिए काम करने वाले लोगों को देते हैं।

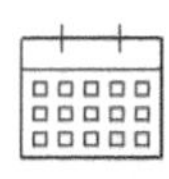 **Date: 2017/06/09**

WOD: *Fugitive*

Pronunciation: फ्यू-जिटिव

Type of word (Category):   *Noun*

English meaning: *a person who has escaped from captivity or is in hiding*

Hindi meaning: भगोड़ा

Synonyms: *escapee, runaway, refugee, absconder, renegade, escaper*

Antonyms: -

English Example: *Fugitive Vijay Mallya's presence at a 'charity dinner' organised by Kohli's foundation forced Indian team to leave early.*

Hindi Example: कोहली के फाउंडेशन द्वारा आयोजित 'चैरिटी डिनर' में भगोड़े विजय माल्या की उपस्थिति ने भारतीय टीम को जल्दी चले जाने के लिए मजबूर किया।

Date: 2017/06/10

WOD: *Mull*

Pronunciation: मल

Type of word (Category):   *Verb*

English meaning: *think about (something) deeply and at length*

Hindi meaning: विचार करना

Synonyms: *ponder, consider, think over/about, contemplate, think, examine*

Antonyms: *ignore, neglect, resolve, forget*

English Example: *Infosys founders are mulling to sell their stake.*

Hindi Example: इन्फोसिस के संस्थापक अपने शेयर बेचने पर विचार रहे हैं।

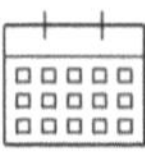 **Date: 2017/06/11**

WOD: *Sublime*

Pronunciation: सब्लाइम

Type of word (Category): Adjective

English meaning: of very great excellence or beauty

Hindi meaning: उत्कृष्ट

Synonyms: exalted, magnificent, glorious, supreme, excellent, outstanding, superb, splendid

Antonyms: lowly, poor, bad, humiliating, secondary

English Example: Rohan Bopanna and Dabrowski showed their sublime performance to win the French Open mixed doubles title.

Hindi Example: रोहन बोपन्ना और डाब्रोन्स्की ने फ्रेंच ओपन मिश्रित युगल खिताब जीतने के लिए अपना उत्कृष्ट प्रदर्शन दिखाया।

Date: 2017/06/12

WOD: *Demure*

Pronunciation: डिम्युअ

Type of word (Category): Adjective

English meaning: (of a woman or her behaviour) reserved, modest, and shy

Hindi meaning: शान्त

Synonyms: modest, meek, mild, reserved, shy, bashful, coy, diffident

Antonyms: bold, aggressive, arrogant, brazen, audacious, impudent

English Example: After playing a role of demure wife in 'English Vinglish', Sridevi is all set to return with a thrilling film 'Mom'.

Hindi Example: 'इंग्लिश विंग्लिश' में शान्त पत्नी की भूमिका निभाने के बाद, श्रीदेवी एक रोमांचक फिल्म 'माँ' के साथ वापस आने के लिए तैयार हैं।

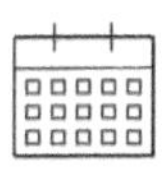

Date: 2017/06/13

WOD: *Perseverance*

Pronunciation: पॅःसि-व्रिअरॅन्स

Type of word (Category):   *Noun*

English meaning: *persistence in doing something despite difficulty or delay in achieving success*

Hindi meaning: दृढ़ता

Synonyms: *persistence, determination, tenacity, resolution, resolve, endurance*

Antonyms: *laziness, idleness, inconstancy, hesitation*

English Example: *Mathematician Anand Kumar attributed the success of Super 30 to the perseverance of students.*

Hindi Example: गणितज्ञ आनंद कुमार ने छात्रों की दृढ़ता को सुपर 30 की सफलता का श्रेय दिया।

Date: 2017/06/14

WOD: *Lineage*

Pronunciation: लिनीअज

Type of word (Category):   *Noun*

English meaning: *direct descent from an ancestor; ancestry or pedigree*

Hindi meaning: वंश

Synonyms: *ancestry, family, descent, derivation, heritage, dynasty, parentage*

Antonyms: *predecessor, extraction, antecedent*

English Example: *Manisha Koirala, despite having a political lineage, prefers to keep a distance from politics.*

Hindi Example: मनीषा कोईराला, राजनीतिक वंश की होने के बावजूद, राजनीति से दूरी रखना पसंद करती हैं।

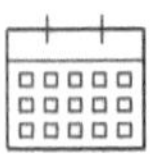 **Date: 2017/06/15**

WOD: *Backlash*

Pronunciation: बैक्ल‍ैश

Type of word (Category): Noun

English meaning: a strong negative reaction by a large number of people, especially to a social or political development

Hindi meaning: प्रतिघात

Synonyms: backfire, retaliation, reaction, repercussion, response, retaliation

Antonyms: -

English Example: After social media backlash, Latif has uploaded a new video saying Sehwag is a great player.

Hindi Example: सोशल मीडिया के प्रतिघात के बाद, लतीफ ने एक नया वीडियो अपलोड किया है जिसमें कहा गया है कि सहवाग एक महान खिलाड़ी है।

Date: 2017/06/16

WOD: *Rebate*

Pronunciation: री-बेट

Type of word (Category): Noun

English meaning: a deduction or discount on a sum of money due

Hindi meaning: छूट

Synonyms: discount, deduction, reduction, allowance, refund, concession

Antonyms: increase, rise

English Example: Dealers are offering rebates on goods to cash in on GST worries.

Hindi Example: डीलर जीएसटी चिंताओं को भुनाने के लिए बहुत सी वस्तुओं पर छूट दे रहे हैं।

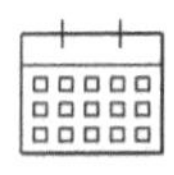 **Date: 2017/06/17**

WOD: *Lopsided*

Pronunciation: लाप्साइडिड

Type of word (Category): Adjective

English meaning: with one side lower or smaller than the other; not equally balanced

Hindi meaning: एकतरफ़ा

Synonyms: uneven, unequal, unbalanced, irregular, one-sided

Antonyms: balanced, even, equal, proportionate

English Example: India defeated Bangladesh by nine wickets in an almost lopsided semi-final.

Hindi Example: भारत ने बांग्लादेश को लगभग एकतरफ़ा सेमीफाइनल में नौ विकेट से पराजित किया।

Date: 2017/06/18

WOD: *Incompetent*

Pronunciation: इन्काम्पिटन्ट

Type of word (Category): Adjective

English meaning: not having the ability to do something as it should be done

Hindi meaning: अक्षम

Synonyms: inept, incapable, ineffective, inefficient, unqualified, unskilled, inexpert, unfit

Antonyms: able, competent, effective, efficient, capable

English Example: Salman Khan said that he felt 'incompetent as an actor' in front of Sunil Grover.

Hindi Example: सलमान खान ने कहा कि उन्होंने सुनील ग्रोवर के सामने 'एक अभिनेता के रूप में अक्षम' महसूस किया।

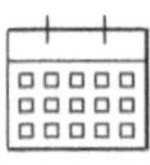 **Date: 2017/06/19**

WOD: *Accelerate*

Pronunciation: ऐक्सेलॅरेट

Type of word (Category):   Verb

English meaning: to happen or make something happen sooner or faster

Hindi meaning: गति बढ़ाना

Synonyms: hasten, expedite, speed, speed up, promote, boost

Antonyms: delay, discourage, halt, stop, slow

English Example: Government is targeting 146 districts to accelerate India's population control drive.

Hindi Example: सरकार भारत की जनसंख्या नियंत्रण अभियान की गति बढ़ाने के लिए 146 जिलों को लक्ष्य बना रही है।

Date: 2017/06/20

WOD: *Condole*

Pronunciation: कन्डोल

Type of word (Category):   Verb

English meaning: express sympathy for (someone); grieve with

Hindi meaning: शोक प्रकट करना

Synonyms: pity, console, sympathize, lament, compassionate, commiserate

Antonyms: exults, revels, rejoices

English Example: Indian hockey team wore black arm bands during its match against Pakistan to condole the deaths of martyrs.

Hindi Example: शहीदों की मौत का शोक प्रकट करने के लिए पाकिस्तान के खिलाफ मैच के दौरान भारतीय हॉकी टीम ने काला आर्म बैंड पहना था।

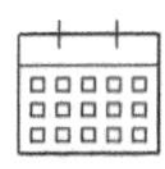
Date: 2017/06/21

WOD: *Candidature*

Pronunciation: कैन्डिडचर

Type of word (Category):   *Noun*

English meaning: *the fact of being a candidate in an election*

Hindi meaning: उम्मीदवारी

Synonyms: *candidacy, electioneering, campaigning, canvassing, nomination, candidate*

Antonyms: -

English Example: *Bihar CM Nitish Kumar expressed happiness over Governor Ram Nath Kovind's candidature for the President's post.*

Hindi Example: बिहार के मुख्यमंत्री नीतीश कुमार ने राष्ट्रपति पद के लिए राज्यपाल रामनाथ कोविंद की उम्मीदवारी पर खुशी जाहिर की।

Date: 2017/06/22

WOD: *Analogy*

Pronunciation: अ-नेलजी

Type of word (Category):   *Noun*

English meaning: *a comparison between things that have similar features, often used to help explain a principle or idea*

Hindi meaning: समानता

Synonyms: *similarity, simile, parallel, parallelism, likeness, correspondence*

Antonyms: *unlikeness, contrast, difference, dissimilarity*

English Example: *PM Narendra Modi explained the importance of Yoga using an analogy of salt.*

Hindi Example: प्रधान मंत्री नरेंद्र मोदी ने योग का महत्व नमक की समानता के प्रयोग से समझाया।

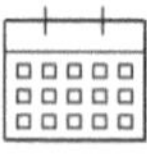 **Date: 2017/06/23**

WOD: *Untenable*

Pronunciation: अन्टेनबल

Type of word (Category):   Adjective

English meaning: (especially of a position or view) not able to be maintained or defended against attack or objection

Hindi meaning: असमर्थनीय

Synonyms: indefensible, unjustifiable, illogical, invalid, baseless, unjustified, refutable, unacceptable

Antonyms: defensible, reasonable, sustainable, justifiable, logical

English Example: Kumble resigned from the post of head coach of Indian cricket team as partnership with Kohli became 'untenable'.

Hindi Example: कुंबले ने भारतीय क्रिकेट टीम के मुख्य कोच के पद से इस्तीफा दे दिया क्योंकि कोहली के साथ साझेदारी 'असमर्थनीय' हो गई थी।

Date: 2017/06/24

WOD: *Infuse*

Pronunciation: इन्फ्यूज़

Type of word (Category):   Verb

English meaning: to fill someone or something with an emotion or quality

Hindi meaning: भर देना

Synonyms: fill, pervade, permeate, suffuse, instill, ingrain

Antonyms: dry, deprive, divest, empty

English Example: The child actor Matin Rey Tangu really infused the film Tubelight with a glow.

Hindi Example: बाल अभिनेता मटीन रे तंगू ने फिल्म ट्यूबलाइट को वास्तव में चमक दमक से भर दिया।

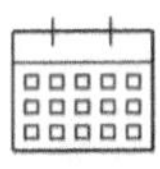 **Date: 2017/06/25**

WOD: *Surpass*

Pronunciation: सॅ-पास

Type of word (Category):   *Verb*

English meaning: *exceed, be greater than*

Hindi meaning: मात कर देना

Synonyms: *excel, exceed, outdo, transcend, outshine, overshadow, beat, outstrip*

Antonyms: *fail, lose, fall behind, surrender*

English Example: *India's population could surpass China's population around 2024.*

Hindi Example: भारत की आबादी 2024 के आसपास चीन की आबादी को मात कर सकती है।

Date: 2017/06/26

WOD: *Unifying*

Pronunciation: यूनफाइइंग

Type of word (Category):   *Adjective*

English meaning: *combining into a single unit*

Hindi meaning: एक करने वाला

Synonyms: *centripetal, integrating, consolidative, integrative*

Antonyms: *disintegrative, divide, separate, disconnect*

English Example: *Amitabh Bachchan explained GST as an unifying force just like the three colours in the national flag.*

Hindi Example: अमिताभ बच्चन ने जीएसटी को राष्ट्रीय ध्वज के तीन रंगों की तरह एक करने वाले बल के रूप में बताया।

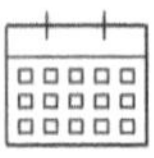 **Date: 2017/06/27**

WOD: *Incessantly*

Pronunciation: इन्सेसन्ट्ली

Type of word (Category): *Adverb*

English meaning: *without interruption, constantly*

Hindi meaning: लगातार

Synonyms: *endlessly, continuously, constantly, ceaselessly, uninterruptedly*

Antonyms: *occasionally, sometimes, seldom, briefly, infrequently*

English Example: *Ranbir Kapoor and Katrina Kaif are incessantly promoting their upcoming film Jagga Jasoos.*

Hindi Example: रणबीर कपूर और कैटरीना कैफ अपनी आगामी फिल्म 'जग्गा जासूस' का लगातार प्रचार कर रहे हैं।

Date: 2017/06/28

WOD: *Hone*

Pronunciation: होन

Type of word (Category): *Verb*

English meaning: *refine or perfect (something) over a period of time*

Hindi meaning: प्रखर करना

Synonyms: *perfect, better, polish, improve, optimise, brush up*

Antonyms: *worsen, debase*

English Example: *Pullela Gopichand honed Kidambi's talent into a top-notch player.*

Hindi Example: पुल्लेला गोपीचंद ने किदांबी की प्रतिभा को शीर्ष पायदान के खिलाड़ी के रूप में प्रखर किया।

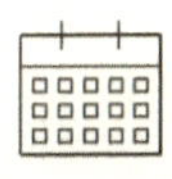 **Date: 2017/06/29**

WOD: *Tackle*

Pronunciation: टेकल

Type of word (Category): *Verb*

English meaning: *make determined efforts to deal with (a problem or difficult task)*

Hindi meaning: निपटना

Synonyms: *undertake, handle, manage, take on, attempt, deal with*

Antonyms: *avoid, neglect, evade, dodge*

English Example: *Government set up 'War room' to tackle GST crises.*

Hindi Example: जीएसटी संकट से निपटने के लिए सरकार ने 'वॉर रूम' की स्थापना की।

Date: 2017/06/30

WOD: *Counterpart*

Pronunciation: काउन्टपार्ट

Type of word (Category): *Noun*

English meaning: *a person or thing that corresponds to or has the same function as another person or thing in a different place or situation*

Hindi meaning: प्रतिरूप

Synonyms: *equivalent, peer, equal, mate, fellow, parallel*

Antonyms: *converse, opposite, reverse*

English Example: *PM Narendra Modi got a bicycle as gift from his Dutch counterpart Mark Rutte.*

Hindi Example: प्रधान मंत्री नरेंद्र मोदी ने अपने डच प्रतिरूप मार्क रूट से उपहार के रूप में एक साइकिल प्राप्त की।

July 2017

Date: 2017/07/01

WOD: *Scintillating*

Pronunciation: सिनटी-लेटिंग

Type of word (Category):   Adjective

English meaning: brilliantly and excitingly clever or skilful

Hindi meaning: बहुत शानदार

Synonyms: brilliant, dazzling, exciting, sparkling, vibrant, effervescent

Antonyms: dull, drab, dumb

English Example: Opener Smriti's scintillating unbeaten 106 runs helped India to win against West Indies.

Hindi Example: सलामी बल्लेबाज स्मृती के बहुत शानदार नाबाद 106 रनों ने भारत को वेस्टइंडीज के खिलाफ जीतने में मदद की।

Date: 2017/07/02

WOD: *Closure*

Pronunciation: क्लोज़र

Type of word (Category):   Noun

English meaning: an act or process of closing something, the fact of a business, organization, etc. stopping operating

Hindi meaning: बंद होना

Synonyms: shutdown, stoppage, barrier, cessation, end, stopper, closing

Antonyms: opening, start, beginning, commencement

English Example: The closure of 43 out of 55 McDonald's outlets in Delhi will hurt almost 1,700 people.

Hindi Example: दिल्ली में 55 मैकडॉनल्ड्स के आउटलेट्स में 43 का बंद होना करीब 1,700 लोगों को नुकसान पहुंचाएगा।

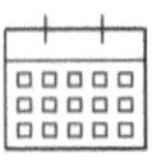

WOD: *Pomp*

Pronunciation: पॉम्प

Type of word (Category): Noun

English meaning: ceremony and splendid display

Hindi meaning: धूमधाम

Synonyms: display, show, magnificence, grandeur, flourish, ostentation, pageant, spectacle

Antonyms: simplicity, plainness, abatement, sarcasm

English Example: After a lot of pomp and fun, Manushi Chhillar from Haryana was crowned Miss India 2017.

Hindi Example: बहुत सारे धूमधाम और मज़े के बाद, हरियाणा की मानुषी छिल्लर को मिस इंडिया 2017 का ताज पहनाया गया।

Date: 2017/07/04

WOD: *Counterfeit*

Pronunciation: काउन्टर्फ़िट

Type of word (Category): Verb

English meaning: make a copy of with the intent to deceive

Hindi meaning: जालसाज़ी करना

Synonyms: fake, forge, copy, reproduce, replicate, imitate, simulate, falsify

Antonyms: true, real, actual, genuine, good

English Example: Allegedly, the new Rs. 200 notes will carry advanced security features to prevent counterfeiting.

Hindi Example: कथित रूप से, 200 रु के नए नोटों में जालसाज़ी करने से रोकने के लिए उन्नत सुरक्षा सुविधाएं मौजूद होंगी।

Date: 2017/07/05

WOD: *Spearhead*

Pronunciation: स्पीर्हेड

Type of word (Category): *Verb*

English meaning: *to lead a course of action*

Hindi meaning: नेतृत्व करना

Synonyms: *pioneer, initiate, command, precede, pilot*

Antonyms: *follow, assist, obey, abide*

English Example: *Former UN Secretary-general praised Prime Minister Modi for spearheading many global initiatives.*

Hindi Example: संयुक्त राष्ट्र के पूर्व महासचिव ने कई विश्वव्यापी प्रस्तावों का नेतृत्व करने के लिए प्रधान मंत्री मोदी की प्रशंसा की।

Date: 2017/07/06

WOD: *Tutelage*

Pronunciation: ट्यूटिलिज

Type of word (Category): *Noun*

English meaning: *protection, backing, or support of a particular person or organization*

Hindi meaning: संरक्षण

Synonyms: *guardianship, aegis, auspices, care*

Antonyms: *ignorance, negligence, indifference*

English Example: *Arjun Kapoor is eager to work under the tutelage and vision of Dibakar Banerjee.*

Hindi Example: अर्जुन कपूर दिबाकर बैनर्जी के संरक्षण और दृष्टीकोण के तहत काम करने के लिए उत्सुक हैं।

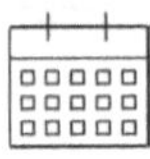 **Date: 2017/07/07**

WOD: *Demit*

Pronunciation: डिमिट

Type of word (Category): *Verb*

English meaning: *to give up a job or position by telling your employer that you are leaving*

Hindi meaning: पदत्याग करना

Synonyms: *resign, relinquish, abdicate, renounce*

Antonyms: *occupy, claim, assert, retain*

English Example: *Chief Election Commissioner Nasim Zaidi demitted office yesterday.*

Hindi Example: मुख्य निर्वाचन आयुक्त नसीम ज़ैदी ने कल कार्यालय से पदत्याग कर दिया।

Date: 2017/07/08

WOD: *Clinch*

Pronunciation: क्लिन्च

Type of word (Category): *Verb*

English meaning: *to finally get or win something*

Hindi meaning: हासिल करना

Synonyms: *grasp, secure, seize, clamp*

Antonyms: *let go, lose, extricate, mislay*

English Example: *India clinched seventh successive ODI series win against West Indies.*

Hindi Example: भारत ने वेस्ट इंडीज के खिलाफ लगातार सातवीं एकदिवसीय जीत हासिल की।

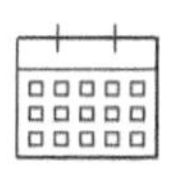
Date: 2017/07/09

WOD: *Valour*

Pronunciation: वैलर

Type of word (Category): Noun

English meaning: exceptional or heroic courage when facing danger (especially in battle)

Hindi meaning: वीरता

Synonyms: prowess, gallantry, pluck, fortitude

Antonyms: cowardice, timidity, poltroonery, effeminacy

English Example: Sridevi's newly released film 'MOM' has showcased the valour of a woman.

Hindi Example: श्रीदेवी की नई फिल्म 'मॉम' ने एक महिला की वीरता का प्रदर्शन किया है।

Date: 2017/07/10

WOD: *Unveil*

Pronunciation: अनवेल

Type of word (Category): Verb

English meaning: remove a veil or covering from, in particular uncover (a new monument or work of art) as part of a public ceremony

Hindi meaning: अनावरण करना

Synonyms: reveal, unmask, bare, expose

Antonyms: conceal, disguise, enshroud, cloak

English Example: A wax statue of actor Ranveer Singh was unveiled at the Grévin wax museum in Paris.

Hindi Example: पेरिस के ग्रैविन मोम संग्रहालय में अभिनेता रणवीर सिंह की एक मोम प्रतिमा का अनावरण किया गया।

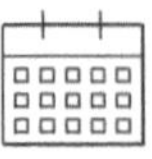 **Date: 2017/07/11**

WOD: *Combat*

Pronunciation: कॉम्बैट

Type of word (Category): Verb

English meaning: To take action to reduce, destroy, or prevent something undesirable

Hindi meaning: निपटना

Synonyms: tackle, withstand, halt, curb

Antonyms: avoid, dodge, elude, evade

English Example: DMRC is planning to add 200 new coaches to combat rush on Delhi Metro lines.

Hindi Example: दिल्ली मेट्रो लाइनों पर भीड़ से निपटने के लिए डीएमआरसी 200 नए कोच जोड़ने की योजना बना रहा है।

Date: 2017/07/12

WOD: *Obligatory*

Pronunciation: अब्लिगट्री

Type of word (Category): Adjective

English meaning: Compulsory or required to do by rule or law

Hindi meaning: अनिवार्य

Synonyms: mandatory, requisite, binding, imperative

Antonyms: optional, discretionary, voluntary, unbidden

English Example: Activities like yoga are now obligatory for engineering students to get a degree.

Hindi Example: योग जैसी गतिविधियां अब इंजीनियरिंग छात्रों को डिग्री प्राप्त करने के लिए अनिवार्य हैं।

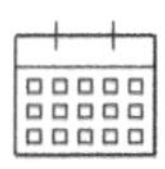 **Date: 2017/07/13**

WOD: *Rubbish*

Pronunciation: रबिश

Type of word (Category): *Verb*

English meaning: *to reject as worthless or to criticize*

Hindi meaning: खारिज करना

Synonyms: *dismiss, discard, rule out, deny*

Antonyms: *admit, concede, acknowledge, avow*

English Example: *After rubbishing the reports first, BCCI later confirmed the formal appointment of Ravi Shastri as Team India's head coach.*

Hindi Example: पहले रिपोर्ट्स को खारिज करने के बाद, बीसीसीआई ने भारतीय टीम के मुख्य कोच के रूप में रवि शास्त्री की औपचारिक नियुक्ति की पुष्टि की।

Date: 2017/07/14

WOD: *Iconic*

Pronunciation: आइकौनिक

Type of word (Category): *Adjective*

English meaning: *widely recognised and popular for its distinctive excellence*

Hindi meaning: प्रतिष्ठित

Synonyms: *renowned, symbolic, legendary, classic*

Antonyms: *unknown, obscure, anonymous, atypical*

English Example: *The 18th IIFA awards ceremony will be held at the iconic MetLife Stadium in New York City.*

Hindi Example: 18वां IIFA पुरस्कार समारोह न्यूयॉर्क शहर के प्रतिष्ठित मेटलाइफ स्टेडियम में आयोजित किया जाएगा।

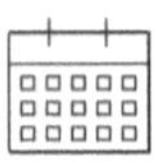 **Date: 2017/07/15**

WOD: *Dupe*

Pronunciation: ड्यूप

Type of word (Category):   *Verb*

English meaning: *to cheat or trick someone*

Hindi meaning: ठगना

Synonyms: *deceive, mislead, delude, con*

Antonyms: *assist, be honest, abide, bestow*

English Example: *5 Delhi traffic policemen were suspended for duping truck drivers in the name of GST.*

Hindi Example: GST के नाम पर ट्रक ड्राइवरों को ठगने के लिए दिल्ली यातायात पुलिस के 5 कर्मचारी निलंबित किये गए।

Date: 2017/07/16

WOD: *Nepotism*

Pronunciation: नैपटिज़म

Type of word (Category):   *Noun*

English meaning: *the act of using your power or influence to get good jobs or unfair advantages for members of your own family*

Hindi meaning: भाई भतीजावाद

Synonyms: *bias, partiality, favouritism, partisanship*

Antonyms: *neutrality, fairness, equity, nonpartisanship*

English Example: *Ranbir Kapoor admitted that he is a product of nepotism that exists in the film industry.*

Hindi Example: रणबीर कपूर ने स्वीकार किया कि वह फिल्म उद्योग में मौजूद भाई-भतीजावाद का एक उत्पाद है।

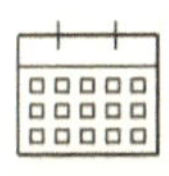 **Date: 2017/07/17**

WOD: *Submerge*

Pronunciation: सबमर्ज

Type of word (Category): *Verb*

English meaning: *to go under water or to make something go below the surface of water*

Hindi meaning: डूब जाना

Synonyms: *swamp, immerse, sink, inundate*

Antonyms: *resurface, emerge, float, swim*

English Example: *More than 75% of Kaziranga National Park has been submerged in flood waters.*

Hindi Example: काज़ीरंगा राष्ट्रीय उद्यान का 75% से अधिक हिस्सा बाढ़ के पानी में डूब गया है।

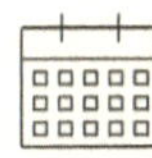 **Date: 2017/07/18**

WOD: *Outrageous*

Pronunciation: आउट्रेजस

Type of word (Category): *Adjective*

English meaning: *very bold and unusual and rather shocking*

Hindi meaning: चौंका देने वाला

Synonyms: *startling, striking, ostentatious, brash, unspeakable, shocking*

Antonyms: *inconspicuous, acceptable, justifiable, reasonable*

English Example: *Roger Federer's outrageous Wimbledon win marks his place in tennis and sporting history.*

Hindi Example: रोजर फेडरर की चौंका देने वाली विंबलडन जीत टेनिस और खेल इतिहास में अपनी जगह बनाती है।

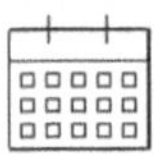 **Date: 2017/07/19**

WOD: *Elan*

Pronunciation: ऐ-लान

Type of word (Category): Noun

English meaning: vigorous spirit or enthusiasm

Hindi meaning: जोश

Synonyms: liveliness, gracefulness, fanaticism, vigour, energy, sprightliness, zest, sparkle

Antonyms: lethargy, apathy, ennui, motionlessness

English Example: IIFA 2017 ended in elan and style.

Hindi Example: IIFA 2017 जोश और अंदाज़ में समाप्त हुआ।

Date: 2017/07/20

WOD: *Constrain*

Pronunciation: कन्स्ट्रेन

Type of word (Category): Verb

English meaning: severely restrict the scope, extent, or activity of

Hindi meaning: रोकना

Synonyms: restrict, limit, curb, check, restrain, regulate

Antonyms: allow, encourage, permit, liberate

English Example: The RBI has clarified that the PCA is not intended to constrain normal operations of the banks for the general public.

Hindi Example: भारतीय रिज़र्व बैंक ने स्पष्ट किया है कि पीसीए का उद्देश्य आम जनता के लिए बैंकों के सामान्य संचालन को रोकना नहीं है।

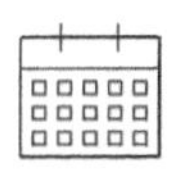 **Date: 2017/07/21**

WOD: *Occupant*

Pronunciation: ऑक्यूपॅन्ट

Type of word (Category): Noun

English meaning: a person who lives or works in a room or building

Hindi meaning: निवासी

Synonyms: resident, inhabitant, denizen, tenant, lodger

Antonyms: visitor, guest, tourist, nonresident

English Example: Ram Nath Kovind will be the next occupant of the Rashtrapati Bhawan.

Hindi Example: रामनाथ कोविंद राष्ट्रपति भवन के अगले निवासी होंगे।

Date: 2017/07/22

WOD: *Embellish*

Pronunciation: एम्बेलिश

Type of word (Category): Verb

English meaning: make (something) more attractive by the addition of decorative details or features

Hindi meaning: सुशोभित करना

Synonyms: decorate, adorn, furnish, beautify, enhance, enrich

Antonyms: uglify, deface, blemish, disfigure

English Example: Harmanpreet's third ODI century was embellished with 20 fours and seven sixes.

Hindi Example: हरमनप्रीत का तीसरा एक दिवसीय शतक 20 चौकों और सात छक्के से सुशोभित था।

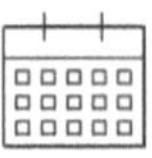 **Date: 2017/07/23**

WOD: *Inundate*

Pronunciation: इन्-अन्डेट

Type of word (Category): *Verb*

English meaning: *to flood an area with water*

Hindi meaning: जलमग्न कर देना

Synonyms: *flood, deluge, overflow, submerge, drench, immerse*

Antonyms: *dry, drain*

English Example: *Heavy rain inundated many roads in Hyderabad.*

Hindi Example: भारी बारिश ने हैदराबाद में कई सड़कों को जलमग्न कर दिया।

Date: 2017/07/24

WOD: *Slapstick*

Pronunciation: स्लेप्स्टिक

Type of word (Category): *Noun*

English meaning: *comedy based on deliberately clumsy actions and humorously embarrassing events*

Hindi meaning: हँसी मज़ाक

Synonyms: *buffoonery, clownery, clowning, foolery, high jinks*

Antonyms: *tragedy*

English Example: *New comedy show, The Drama Company, is all about slapstick comedy.*

Hindi Example: नया कॉमेडी शो, द ड्रामा कंपनी, हँसी मज़ाक की कॉमेडी के बारे में है।

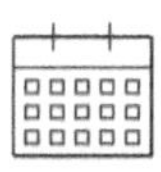 **Date: 2017/07/25**

WOD: *Daunt*

Pronunciation: डॉन्ट

Type of word (Category): Verb

English meaning: to make someone feel slightly frightened or worried about their ability to achieve something

Hindi meaning: भयभीत करना

Synonyms: frighten, discourage, intimidate, dishearten, dismay, scare

Antonyms: stimulate, encourage, incite, embolden

English Example: Ranbir Kapoor, who is playing Sanjay Dutt's role in the movie, said doing the biopic was daunting initially.

Hindi Example: रणबीर कपूर, जो फिल्म में संजय दत्त की भूमिका निभा रहे हैं, ने कहा कि पहली बार जीवनी फिल्म करना भयभीत करने वाला था।

Date: 2017/07/26

WOD: *Skyrocket*

Pronunciation: स्काइराकट

Type of word (Category): Verb

English meaning: (of a price, rate, or amount) increase very steeply or rapidly

Hindi meaning: बढ़ना

Synonyms: shoot up, zoom, arise, escalate, rise, increase

Antonyms: crash, collapse, come down, ascend

English Example: The price of tomatoes in Delhi's retail market has skyrocketed to Rs 100 per kg.

Hindi Example: दिल्ली के खुदरा बाजार में टमाटर की कीमत 100 रुपये प्रति किलो तक बढ़ गई है।

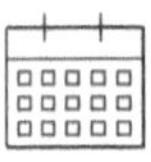 **Date: 2017/07/27**

WOD: *Prowess*

Pronunciation: प्राउअस

Type of word (Category):   Noun

English meaning: bravery in battle

Hindi meaning: कौशल

Synonyms: valor, courage, bravery, heroism, intrepidity, gallantry

Antonyms: inability, powerlessness, cowardice

English Example: Kargil Vijay Diwas reminds us of India's military prowess and the great sacrifices made by the armed forces.

Hindi Example: कारगिल विजय दिवस हमें भारत के सैन्य कौशल और सशस्त्र बलों द्वारा दिए गए महान बलिदान की याद दिलाता है।

Date: 2017/07/28

WOD: *Vivacious*

Pronunciation: वि-वेशस

Type of word (Category):   Adjective

English meaning: (especially of a woman) attractively lively and animated

Hindi meaning: ज़िंदादिल

Synonyms: lively, spirited, effervescent, bubbly, ebullient, buoyant, joyful, cheerful

Antonyms: dull, lifeless, spiritless, indolent

English Example: Young and vivacious Disha Patani added glamour to the Manav Gangwani's show at the India Couture Week 2017.

Hindi Example: युवा और ज़िंदादिल दिशा पटानी ने इंडिया कोउचर वीक 2017 में मानव गंगवानी के शो में ग्लैमर को जोड़ा।

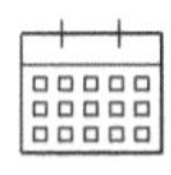

Date: 2017/07/29

WOD: *Dispel*

Pronunciation: डिस्पेल

Type of word (Category): *Verb*

English meaning: *make (a doubt, feeling, or belief) disappear*

Hindi meaning: (संदेह) दूर करना

Synonyms: *eliminate, dismiss, dissipate, disperse, disseminate*

Antonyms: *accumulate, accept, gather, appear*

English Example: *Hardik Pandya dispelled doubts over his Test capabilities by scoring fifty runs in his debut match in Galle.*

Hindi Example: हार्दिक पंड्या ने गॉल में अपने डेब्यू मैच में पचास रन हासिल कर अपनी टेस्ट क्षमताओं पर संदेह को दूर किया।

Date: 2017/07/30

WOD: *Enthrall*

Pronunciation: एन्थ्रॉल

Type of word (Category): *Verb*

English meaning: *capture the fascinated attention of*

Hindi meaning: मंत्रमुग्ध करना

Synonyms: *captivate, engross, enchant, fascinate, enrapture, attract*

Antonyms: *bore, disenchant, weary, dull*

English Example: *Pro Kabaddi League's fifth season is all set to enthrall the fans.*

Hindi Example: प्रो कबड्डी लीग का पांचवां सीजन प्रशंसकों को मंत्रमुग्ध करने के लिए तैयार है।

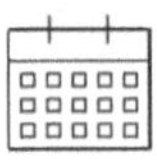 **Date: 2017/07/31**

WOD: *Opportune*

Pronunciation: आपर्टून

Type of word (Category): Adjective

English meaning: (of a time) especially convenient or appropriate for a particular action or event

Hindi meaning: उपयुक्त

Synonyms: timely, propitious, favourable, apt, appropriate

Antonyms: unsuitable, inopportune, untimely, inappropriate

English Example: Bihar CM Nitish Kumar said that he will give a befitting reply to all at an opportune time.

Hindi Example: बिहार के मुख्यमंत्री नीतीश कुमार ने कहा कि वह उपयुक्त समय पर सभी को उचित उत्तर देंगे।

August 2017

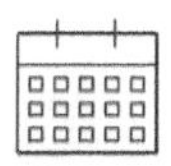

Date: 2017/08/01

WOD: *Hinge*

Pronunciation: हिन्ज

Type of word (Category): *Verb*

English meaning: depend entirely on, a circumstance upon which subsequent events depend

Hindi meaning: निर्भर होना

Synonyms: *depend, hang, rest, be based, be dependent*

Antonyms: *disconnect*

English Example: *ICC's dream of cricket in Olympics hinges on India.*

Hindi Example: ओलंपिक में आईसीसी के क्रिकेट का सपना भारत पर निर्भर है।

Date: 2017/08/02

WOD: *Uproar*

Pronunciation: अप्रॉर

Type of word (Category): *Noun*

English meaning: *a loud and impassioned noise or disturbance*

Hindi meaning: शोरगुल

Synonyms: *tumult, disturbance, commotion, turmoil, ruckus, disorder*

Antonyms: *peace, calm, agreement, serenity*

English Example: *There was an uproar in Rajya Sabha over govt decision to roll back LPG subsidy.*

Hindi Example: एलपीजी सब्सिडी घटाने के सरकार के फैसले पर राज्यसभा में शोरगुल हुआ।

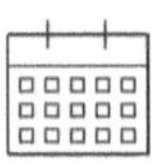 **Date: 2017/08/03**

WOD: *Staggering*

Pronunciation: स्टैगरिंग

Type of word (Category): Adjective

English meaning: very shocking and surprising

Hindi meaning: आश्चर्यजनक

Synonyms: astonishing, mind-boggling, breathtaking, shocking

Antonyms: unremarkable, discouraging, disheartening, exhausting

English Example: RIL chairman Mukesh Ambani recorded a staggering increase of USD 12.1 billion in his wealth this year.

Hindi Example: रिलायंस इंडस्ट्रीज के चेयरमैन मुकेश अंबानी ने इस साल अपनी संपत्ति में 12.1 अरब डॉलर की आश्चर्यजनक बढ़ोतरी दर्ज की।

Date: 2017/08/04

WOD: *Awestruck*

Pronunciation: ऑ-स्ट्रक

Type of word (Category): Adjective

English meaning: having or showing a feeling of mixed reverence and respect and wonder and dread

Hindi meaning: विस्मयाभिभूत

Synonyms: awed, amazed, astonished, breathless, stunned, agog

Antonyms: unimpressed, disinterested

English Example: Akshay Kumar was awestruck to see the dance talent and the stunts on the reality show Dance +3.

Hindi Example: रियलिटी शो डांस +3 पर डांस प्रतिभा और स्टंट देख कर अक्षय कुमार विस्मयाभिभूत थे।

 **Date: 2017/08/05**

WOD: *Ebullient*

Pronunciation: इ-बल्यन्ट

Type of word (Category): Adjective

English meaning: exuberant, buoyant, enthusiastic, joyful, vivacious, lively

Hindi meaning: जोशीला

Synonyms: cheerful and full of energy

Antonyms: apathetic, spiritless, unenthusiastic, unmotivated

English Example: SRK's ebullient character in 'Jab Harry Met Sejal' may bring further recognition to the tourist guides.

Hindi Example: जब हैरी मेट सेजल' में शाहरुख खान का जोशीला चरित्र, पर्यटक गाइड को और अधिक पहचान प्रदान कर सकता हैं।

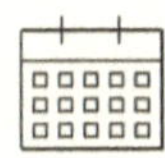 **Date: 2017/08/06**

WOD: *Penchant*

Pronunciation: पेन्चन्ट

Type of word (Category): Noun

English meaning: a strong or habitual liking for something or tendency to do something

Hindi meaning: विशेष रुचि

Synonyms: inclination, liking, fondness, affinity

Antonyms: disinclination, hatred, aversion, antipathy

English Example: Anil Kapoor has penchant for perfection.

Hindi Example: अनिल कपूर की निपुणता के लिए विशेष रुचि है।

 **Date: 2017/08/07**

WOD: *Virtually*

Pronunciation: वर्चूअली

Type of word (Category): Adverb

English meaning: nearly; almost

Hindi meaning: लगभग

Synonyms: almost, nearly, about, substantially, just about

Antonyms: entirely, exactly, absolutely, wholly

English Example: Due to patriotism, Chinese rakhis have virtually disappeared this year from the market.

Hindi Example: देशभक्ति के कारण, इस साल बाजार से चीनी राखी लगभग गायब हो गई हैं।

 **Date: 2017/08/08**

WOD: *Vulnerable*

Pronunciation: वल्नरबल

Type of word (Category): Adjective

English meaning: exposed to the possibility of being attacked or harmed, either physically or emotionally

Hindi meaning: अतिसंवेदनशील

Synonyms: susceptible, hypersensitive, squeamish, highly strung

Antonyms: invulnerable, defensible, secure, unsusceptible

English Example: 29 Indian cities and towns are highly vulnerable to earthquakes.

Hindi Example: 29 भारतीय शहर और कस्बें भूकम्प के लिए अतिसंवेदनशील है।

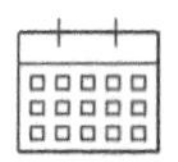

Date: 2017/08/09

WOD: *Clobber*

Pronunciation: क्लॉबर

Type of word (Category):   *Verb*

English meaning: *to defeat completely*

Hindi meaning: बुरी तरह से हराना

Synonyms: *rout, trounce, thrash, wallop, spread-eagle*

Antonyms: *praise, uphold*

English Example: *Kohli and Company clobbered Sri Lanka in Colombo to win the Test series.*

Hindi Example: कोहली एंड कंपनी ने कोलंबो टेस्ट सीरीज जीतने के लिए श्रीलंका को बुरी तरह से हराया।

Date: 2017/08/10

WOD: *Cliffhanger*

Pronunciation: क्लिफहैंगर

Type of word (Category):   *Noun*

English meaning: *a story or a situation that is exciting because its ending or result is uncertain until it happens*

Hindi meaning: रोचक परिस्थिति

Synonyms: *close-call, shocker, thriller, squeaker, suspenseful*

Antonyms: -

English Example: *In Gujarat RS seat cliffhanger, Sonia Gandhi's top advisor Ahmed Patel won at the last moment.*

Hindi Example: गुजरात राज्य सभा सीट की रोचक परिस्थिति में, सोनिया गांधी के शीर्ष सलाहकार अहमद पटेल आखिरी क्षण पर जीतें।

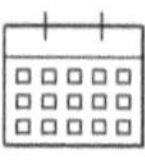 **Date: 2017/08/11**

WOD: *Acrimonious*

Pronunciation: ऐक्रमोनीअस

Type of word (Category): Adjective

English meaning: (typically of speech or discussion) angry and bitter

Hindi meaning: कटुतापूर्ण

Synonyms: bitter, caustic, sarcastic, harsh

Antonyms: kind, agreeable, peaceable, pleasant

English Example: BCCI marked a closure to Anil Kumble's acrimonious episode by clearing the dues.

Hindi Example: बीसीसीआई ने बकाया राशि को चुकता कर अनिल कुंबले के कटुतापूर्ण प्रकरण के समाप्त होने का संकेत दिया।

Date: 2017/08/12

WOD: *Milieu*

Pronunciation: मील्यॅः

Type of word (Category): Noun

English meaning: a person's social environment

Hindi meaning: वातावरण

Synonyms: environment, background, backdrop, setting, surroundings

Antonyms: -

English Example: Director Shree Narayan Singh knows his milieu and holds up a mirror to society in 'Toilet: Ek Prem Katha' movie.

Hindi Example: निर्देशक श्री नारायण सिंह अपने वातावरण को जानते हैं और समाज को 'टॉयलेट: एक प्रेम कथा' फिल्म में एक आइना दिखाते हैं।

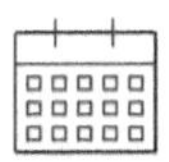 **Date: 2017/08/13**

WOD: *Oratory*

Pronunciation: ऑरॅटॅरि

Type of word (Category):   Noun

English meaning: skilful and effective public speaking

Hindi meaning: वाक्पटुता

Synonyms: rhetoric, elocution, speech-making, declamation, speech

Antonyms: brief friendly chat

English Example: Venkaiah Naidu, known for his oratory skills, took oath as the 13th Vice-President of India.

Hindi Example: वेंकैया नायडू, जो अपने वाक्पटुता कौशल के लिए जाने जाते हैं, ने भारत के 13वें उप-राष्ट्रपति के रूप में शपथ ली।

Date: 2017/08/14

WOD: *Clampdown*

Pronunciation: क्लैम्प्डाउन

Type of word (Category):   Noun

English meaning: a sudden action taken by a government or people in authority to stop or limit a particular activity

Hindi meaning: कठोर नीति

Synonyms: repression, restriction, embargo, suppression

Antonyms: freedom, democracy

English Example: According to recent reports, US may lose its competitive edge due to clampdown on H-1B visa programme.

Hindi Example: हाल की रिपोर्ट के मुताबिक, एच -1 बी वीजा कार्यक्रम पर कठोर नीति के कारण अमेरिका अपनी प्रतिस्पर्धा की तीव्रता को खो सकता है।

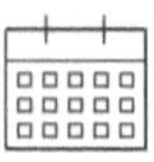 **Date: 2017/08/15**

WOD: *Bygone*

Pronunciation: बाइगॉन

Type of word (Category): Adjective

English meaning: belonging to an earlier time

Hindi meaning: पुराना

Synonyms: former, past, old, ancient, archaic

Antonyms: new, future, forthcoming, modern

English Example: There's no better place than Old Delhi to get a glimpse of the bygone era on this 15th August.

Hindi Example: इस 15वें अगस्त को पुराने युग की एक झलक पाने के लिए पुरानी दिल्ली की तुलना में कोई और बेहतर जगह नहीं है।

Date: 2017/08/16

WOD: *Overarching*

Pronunciation: ओवरार्चिंग

Type of word (Category): Adjective

English meaning: most important, because of including or affecting all other areas

Hindi meaning: अति महत्वपूर्ण

Synonyms: very important, urgent, essential, all-important, top of mind

Antonyms: insignificant, unimportant, trivial, frivolous

English Example: The Supreme Court said that there has to be 'overarching' guidelines to guard personal information in public domain.

Hindi Example: सुप्रीम कोर्ट ने कहा कि सार्वजनिक डोमेन में निजी जानकारी की रक्षा के लिए 'अति महत्वपूर्ण' दिशानिर्देश होने चाहिए।

 **Date: 2017/08/17**

WOD: *Rampart*

Pronunciation: रैम्पार्ट

Type of word (Category): Noun

English meaning: a defensive wall of a castle or walled city, having a broad top with a walkway and typically a stone parapet

Hindi meaning: किले की दीवार

Synonyms: embankment, parapet, breastwork, stockade, outwork, fortification

Antonyms: -

English Example: PM Modi delivered his shortest speech from the ramparts of the historic Red Fort this year.

Hindi Example: प्रधानमंत्री मोदी ने इस साल ऐतिहासिक लाल किले की दीवार से अपना सबसे छोटा भाषण दिया।

Date: 2017/08/18

WOD: *Clamour*

Pronunciation: क्लैमर

Type of word (Category): Noun

English meaning: a loud complaint about something or a demand for something

Hindi meaning: जोरदार माँग

Synonyms: demand, urging, insistence, outcry, complaints, protests

Antonyms: obviate, inactivity, peace

English Example: There is a growing clamour for import restrictions on electronic and IT products from China due to concerns over security.

Hindi Example: सुरक्षा से संबंधित चिंताओं के कारण चीन से इलेक्ट्रॉनिक और आईटी उत्पादों पर आयात प्रतिबंधों के लिए जोरदार माँग बढ़ रही है।

 **Date: 2017/08/19**

WOD: *Guffaw*

Pronunciation: गॅफ़ाः

Type of word (Category): Verb

English meaning: to laugh loudly, especially at something stupid that someone has said or done

Hindi meaning: ठहाका लगाना

Synonyms: belly, laugh, cackle, laugh, giggle, laugh loudly

Antonyms: cry, groan, sob, moan

English Example: Every time you guffaw at the antics of the cast of Bareilly Ki Barfi, you are reminded that there is so much humour in our daily routine.

Hindi Example: हर बार जब आप बरेली की बर्फी के कलाकारों की हरकतों पर ठहाका लगाते हैं, तो आपको याद दिलाया जाता है कि हमारे दैनिक दिनचर्या में भी बहुत अधिक हास्य है।

Date: 2017/08/20

WOD: *Vouch*

Pronunciation: वाउच

Type of word (Category): Verb

English meaning: confirm, affirm, verify, substantiate, prove, endorse

Hindi meaning: प्रमाणित करना

Synonyms: assert or confirm as a result of one's own experience the truth or accuracy of (something)

Antonyms: deny, renounce, reject, refute

English Example: Anyone who has seen Sunil Grover can vouch that he is the best in Gutthi and Dr. Mashoor Gulati's role.

Hindi Example: जिसने भी सुनील ग्रोवर को देखा है, यह प्रमाणित कर सकता है कि वह गुत्थी और डॉ मशहूर गुलाटी की भूमिका में सर्वश्रेष्ठ हैं।

Date: 2017/08/21

WOD: *Taboo*

Pronunciation: टैबू

Type of word (Category): Noun

English meaning: an action or word that is avoided for religious or social reasons

Hindi meaning: वर्जित कार्य

Synonyms: prohibition, proscription, interdiction, interdict, ban, restriction, boycott, non-acceptance

Antonyms: acceptance, encouragement

English Example: Anushka Sharma has refused to advertise products that are considered socially a taboo.

Hindi Example: अनुष्का शर्मा ने उन उत्पादों का विज्ञापन करने से इनकार कर दिया है जिन्हें सामाजिक रूप से वर्जित माना जाता है।

Date: 2017/08/22

WOD: *Jiffy*

Pronunciation: जिफी

Type of word (Category): Noun

English meaning: a very short time; a moment

Hindi meaning: पल

Synonyms: very soon, soon, in a moment, shortly, instant, moment aeon, age, eternity, forever

Antonyms: aeon, age, eternity

English Example: Shikhar Dhawan punished the Sri Lankan bowlers and finished the match in a jiffy.

Hindi Example: शिखर धवन ने श्रीलंका के गेंदबाजों को दंडित किया और एक पल में मैच समाप्त कर दिया।

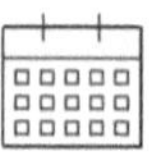

Date: 2017/08/23

WOD: *Marvel*

Pronunciation: मार्वल

Type of word (Category): *Verb*

English meaning: *to show or feel surprise or admiration*

Hindi meaning: आश्चर्य चकित होना

Synonyms: *wonder, stare, gaze, boggle*

Antonyms: *disregard, deride*

English Example: *The first total solar eclipse have marvelled millions of Americans.*

Hindi Example: पहले पूर्ण सूर्य ग्रहण ने लाखों अमेरिकियों को आश्चर्यचकित किया है।

Date: 2017/08/24

WOD: *Confer*

Pronunciation: कन्फर

Type of word (Category): *Verb*

English meaning: *to give an official title, honour, or advantage to someone*

Hindi meaning: प्रदान करना

Synonyms: *give, bestow, present, award, grant*

Antonyms: *taking, deprive, disallow, refuse*

English Example: *Government has decided to confer the Rajiv Gandhi Khel Ratna 2017 to Jhajharia and former hockey captain Sardar Singh.*

Hindi Example: सरकार ने राजीव गांधी खेल रत्न 2017 को झाझरिया और पूर्व हॉकी कप्तान सरदार सिंह को प्रदान करने का फैसला किया है।

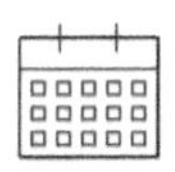 **Date: 2017/08/25**

WOD: *Merriment*

Pronunciation: मेरिमन्ट

Type of word (Category): Noun

English meaning: an occasion when people laugh or have an enjoyable time together; gaiety and fun

Hindi meaning: आनंद

Synonyms: high spirits, exuberance, cheerfulness, gaiety, fun, festivity

Antonyms: boredom, depression, dejection, gloom, sadness

English Example: Ganesh Chaturthi is the time when we are full of excitement and merriment all around us.

Hindi Example: गणेश चतुर्थी एक ऐसा समय है जब हम अपने चारों ओर उत्साह और आनंद से भरे हुए होते हैं।

Date: 2017/08/26

WOD: *Motif*

Pronunciation: मो-टीफ

Type of word (Category): Noun

English meaning: a decorative image or design, especially a repeated one forming a pattern

Hindi meaning: रूपांकन

Synonyms: design, pattern, figure, shape, logo, monogram, emblem, ornament

Antonyms: -

English Example: RBI said the new Rs. 200 note has the motif of Sanchi Stupa on the reverse.

Hindi Example: आरबीआई ने कहा कि नए 200 रुपये के नोट में पीछे के भाग में सांची स्तूप का रूपांकन है।

AUGUST

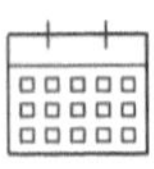 **Date: 2017/08/27**

WOD: *Denigrate*

Pronunciation: डेन्इग्रेट

Type of word (Category): *Verb*

English meaning: *charge falsely or with malicious intent; attack the good name and reputation of someone*

Hindi meaning: नीचा दिखाना

Synonyms: *disparage, diminish, deprecate, decry, criticize unfairly, slander*

Antonyms: *praise, commend, compliment, boost, extol*

English Example: *Harbhajan Singh gave a suitable reply the one who tried to denigrate his English skills.*

Hindi Example: हरभजन सिंह ने एक व्यक्ति को उपयुक्त उत्तर दिया जिसने उनके अंग्रेजी के कौशल को नीचा दिखाने की कोशिश की।

Date: 2017/08/28

WOD: *Intrinsic*

Pronunciation: इन्ट्रिन्सिक

Type of word (Category): *Adjective*

English meaning: *being an extremely important and basic characteristic of a person or thing*

Hindi meaning: मूलभूत

Synonyms: *inherent, essential, congenital, congenital, natural, basic*

Antonyms: *extrinsic, acquired, accidental, external*

English Example: *The Supreme Court has ruled that right to privacy is a fundamental right, it is intrinsic to right to life.*

Hindi Example: सर्वोच्च न्यायालय ने फैसला सुनाया है कि निजता का अधिकार मौलिक अधिकार है, यह जीवन के अधिकार के लिए मूलभूत है।

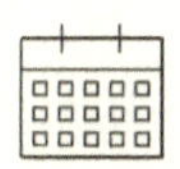

Date: 2017/08/29

WOD: *Slew*

Pronunciation: स्लू

Type of word (Category):   Noun

English meaning: a large number or quantity of something

Hindi meaning: अधिक संख्या

Synonyms: oodles, heap, plurality, many, multitude, lot

Antonyms: handful, smattering, deficiency, dearth

English Example: Dipak Misra sworn in as chief justice of India, inherited slew of challenges.

Hindi Example: दीपक मिश्रा ने भारत के मुख्य न्यायाधीश के रूप में शपथ ली, अधिक संख्या में चुनौतियां विरासत में मिलीं।

Date: 2017/08/30

WOD: *Phenomenal*

Pronunciation: फ़ि-नॉम्इनॅल

Type of word (Category):   Adjective

English meaning: remarkable or exceptional, especially exceptionally good

Hindi meaning: असाधारण

Synonyms: exceptional, extraordinary, remarkable, outstanding, astonishing, astounding

Antonyms: ordinary, normal, regular, average

English Example: August 29 is marked as the birth anniversary of India's phenomenal athlete Major Dhyan Chand.

Hindi Example: 29 अगस्त को भारत के असाधारण एथलीट मेजर ध्यानचंद के जन्मदिवस के रूप में चिह्नित किया गया है।

AUGUST

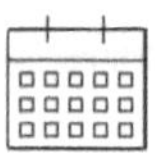 **Date: 2017/08/31**

WOD: *Incessant*

Pronunciation: इन्सेसन्ट

Type of word (Category):   *Adjective*

English meaning: *(of something regarded as unpleasant) continuing without pause or interruption*

Hindi meaning: लगातार

Synonyms: *ceaseless, constant, continual, perpetual, continuous, uninterrupted*

Antonyms: *discontinuous, intermittent, irregular, occasional, ending*

English Example: *Incessant rain in Mumbai over the last two days has paralysed the city.*

Hindi Example: मुंबई में पिछले दो दिनों की लगातार बारिश ने शहर को शक्तिहीन कर दिया है।

नमस्ते! English

Learn English from Hindi

आपको English सिखाने वाला App.

2 Million + Download

100 + Lesson

Learn English from Conversation

Practice Spoken English

Learn English from News

Fun Learning Games

Scan QR code
to download the App

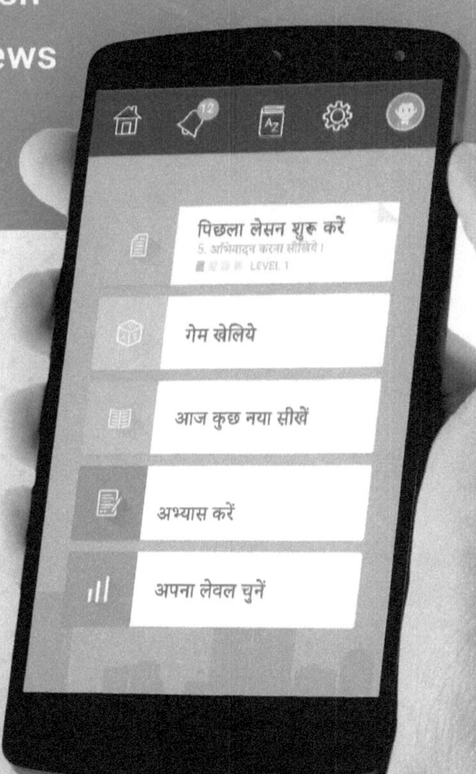

September 2017

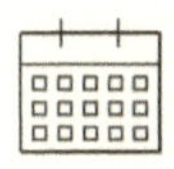 **Date: 2017/09/01**

WOD: *Rookie*

Pronunciation: रुकी

Type of word (Category): Noun

English meaning: a person who is new to an organization or an activity

Hindi meaning: नया सदस्य

Synonyms: beginner, novice, greenhorn, newcomer

Antonyms: professional, old-timer, master, expert

English Example: Indian spinner Kuldeep Yadav feels that Dhoni's influence on rookie bowlers is unparalleled.

Hindi Example: भारतीय स्पिनर कुलदीप यादव का मानना है कि धोनी का प्रभाव नए गेंदबाजों पर अद्वितीय है।

 **Date: 2017/09/02**

WOD: *Aplomb*

Pronunciation: अ-प्लाम

Type of word (Category): Noun

English meaning: self-confidence or assurance, especially when in a demanding situation

Hindi meaning: आत्मविश्वास

Synonyms: self-assurance, composure, poise, self-confidence, imperturbability, equilibrium

Antonyms: fear, anxiety, awkwardness, embarrassment

English Example: Suresh Prabhu performed his duty with aplomb as a Railway Minister.

Hindi Example: सुरेश प्रभु ने रेल मंत्री के रूप में अपने कर्तव्य को आत्मविश्वास के साथ निभाया।

SEPTEMBER

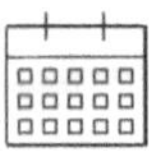 **Date: 2017/09/03**

WOD: *Contentious*

Pronunciation: कन्टेन्शस

Type of word (Category): Adjective

English meaning: causing or likely to cause disagreement

Hindi meaning: विवादपूर्ण

Synonyms: quarrelsome, controversial, disputable, argumentative, ambivalent

Antonyms: agreeable, peaceful, amicable, warmhearted

English Example: Uber chose Expedia's chief Dara Khosrowshahi as CEO after contentious deliberations.

Hindi Example: विवादपूर्ण विचार-विमर्श के बाद उबर ने एक्सपीडिया के प्रमुख दारा खोसरोशाही को सीईओ के रूप में चुना।

Date: 2017/09/04

WOD: *Contemplation*

Pronunciation: कॉन्टॅम्प्लेशॅन

Type of word (Category): Noun

English meaning: the action of looking thoughtfully at something for a long time, deep reflective thought

Hindi meaning: चिंतन

Synonyms: thought, reflection, consideration, examination, inspection, observation

Antonyms: disregard, disdain, neglect, rejection, avoidance

English Example: Around two million Muslims will visit Mount Arafat to spend a day in contemplation this year.

Hindi Example: इस साल लगभग दो लाख मुस्लिम चिंतन में एक दिन व्यतीत करने के लिए माउंट अराफात जाएंगे।

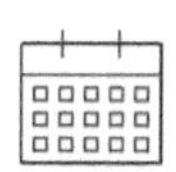 **Date: 2017/09/05**

WOD: *Elevation*

Pronunciation: एलि-वेशन

Type of word (Category):   *Noun*

English meaning: *the action or fact of raising or being raised to a higher or more important level, state, or position*

Hindi meaning: उन्नति

Synonyms: *promotion, upgrading, advancement, advance, preferment*

Antonyms: *demotion, disdain, fall, decline*

English Example: *With her elevation as Defence Minister, Nirmala Sitharaman joins a powerful Cabinet Committee on Security chaired by the PM.*

Hindi Example: रक्षा मंत्री के रूप में अपनी उन्नति के साथ, निर्मला सीतारमण प्रधान मंत्री द्वारा अध्यक्षता वाली सुरक्षा की शक्तिशाली कैबिनेट कमेटी में शामिल हुईं।

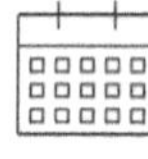 **Date: 2017/09/06**

WOD: *Reiterate*

Pronunciation: री-इटरैट

Type of word (Category):   *Verb*

English meaning: *say something again or a number of times, typically for emphasis or clarity*

Hindi meaning: दोहराना

Synonyms: *repeat, restate, recapitulate, recur, repetition*

Antonyms: *secrete, keep, conceal, hold back*

English Example: *Mr. Modi reiterated his vision for a digital economic and financial system at the 9th BRICS Summit.*

Hindi Example: श्री मोदी ने 9वें ब्रिक्स सम्मेलन में डिजिटल आर्थिक और वित्तीय प्रणाली को लेकर अपने दृष्टिकोण को दोहराया।

SEPTEMBER

 **Date: 2017/09/07**

WOD: *Revel*

Pronunciation: रेवल

Type of word (Category): Verb

English meaning: enjoy oneself in a lively and noisy way, especially with drinking and dancing

Hindi meaning: आनंद लेना

Synonyms: enjoy, relish, delight, celebrate, carouse

Antonyms: grieve, mourn, deplore, dislike

English Example: Kohli wants Team India to revel in unpredictability too.

Hindi Example: कोहली चाहते है कि टीम इंडिया अनिश्चितता में भी आनंद लें।

Date: 2017/09/08

WOD: *Satiate*

Pronunciation: सेशिएट

Type of word (Category): Verb

English meaning: fill to satisfaction   sate

Hindi meaning: तृप्त करना

Synonyms: satisfy, glut, quench, gorge

Antonyms: deprive, insatiate, bereave, starve

English Example: Upasana Singh feels that satiating her creativity as an artiste is more important than money.

Hindi Example: उपासना सिंह मानती है कि एक कलाकार के रूप में अपनी रचनात्मकता को तृप्त करना पैसे से अधिक महत्वपूर्ण है।

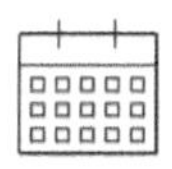 **Date: 2017/09/09**

WOD: *Rung*

Pronunciation: रंग

Type of word (Category): Noun

English meaning: a level in a hierarchical structure, especially a class or career structure

Hindi meaning: पायदान

Synonyms: stage, step, level, rank, position, status

Antonyms:

English Example: Australia slipped one rung to fifth in the latest ICC Test rankings.

Hindi Example: आईसीसी टेस्ट रैंकिंग में ऑस्ट्रेलिया एक पायदान फिसल कर पांचवें स्थान पर पहुंचा।

 **Date: 2017/09/10**

WOD: *Amnesty*

Pronunciation: ऐम्नस्टी

Type of word (Category): Noun

English meaning: an official pardon for people who have been convicted of political offences

Hindi meaning: आम माफ़ी

Synonyms: pardon, reprieve, absolution, forgiveness, acquittal

Antonyms: penalty, punishment, vengeance, adjudication

English Example: US tech giants have pledged to stand by their employees after the Trump administration scrapped an amnesty programme.

Hindi Example: अमेरिकी तकनीकी दिग्गजों ने ट्रम्प प्रशासन के आम माफ़ी कार्यक्रम को समाप्त कर देने के बाद अपने कर्मचारियों के लिए खड़े होने का वादा किया।

 **Date: 2017/09/11**

WOD: *Shrine*

Pronunciation: श्राइन

Type of word (Category): Noun

English meaning: a place of worship hallowed by association with some sacred thing or person

Hindi meaning: तीर्थस्थान

Synonyms: holy place, temple, tabernacle, altar, sanctuary, sanctum

Antonyms: -

English Example: Kailash Mansarovar Yatra ends with record number of pilgrims visiting shrine this year.

Hindi Example: कैलाश मानसरोवर यात्रा इस साल तीर्थस्थान के दर्शन के लिए आने वाले तीर्थ यात्रियों की रिकॉर्ड संख्या के साथ समाप्त हुई है।

Date: 2017/09/12

WOD: *Fleece*

Pronunciation: फ्लीस

Type of word (Category): Verb

English meaning: to take someone's money dishonestly, by charging too much money or by cheating them

Hindi meaning: लूटना

Synonyms: cheat, defraud, overcharge, swindle, gouge

Antonyms: give, offer

English Example: Aadhaar is free, but enrolment centres fleece applicants.

Hindi Example: आधार नि:शुल्क है, लेकिन नामांकन केन्द्र आवेदकों को लूटते हैं।

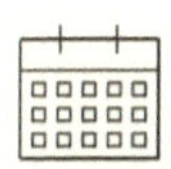 **Date: 2017/09/13**

WOD: *Embark*

Pronunciation: एम्बार्क

Type of word (Category): *Verb*

English meaning: *begin (a course of action)*

Hindi meaning: प्रारम्भ करना

Synonyms: *start, begin, commence, set out, initiate*

Antonyms: *leave, end, conclude, stop, finish*

English Example: *Indian Navy's women team embarked on historic voyage named 'Navika Sagar Parikrama'.*

Hindi Example: भारतीय नौसेना की महिला टीम ने 'नाविका सागर परिक्रमा' नामक ऐतिहासिक यात्रा प्रारम्भ की।

 **Date: 2017/09/14**

WOD: *Robust*

Pronunciation: रो-बस्ट

Type of word (Category): *Adjective*

English meaning: *strong enough to withstand or overcome intellectual challenges or adversity*

Hindi meaning: मज़बूत

Synonyms: *strong, fortified, sturdy, powerful, tough*

Antonyms: *weak, fragile, uncertain, dull*

English Example: *Robust security arrangements have been put in place for the 12th Indo-Japan Summit in Gujarat.*

Hindi Example: गुजरात में 12 वीं भारत-जापान शिखर सम्मेलन के लिए मज़बूत सुरक्षा व्यवस्था की गई है।

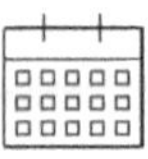 **Date: 2017/09/15**

WOD: *Rile*

Pronunciation: राइल

Type of word (Category): *Verb*

English meaning: *make (someone) annoyed or irritated*

Hindi meaning: गुस्सा दिलाना

Synonyms: *irritate, annoy, bother, provoke, affront, anger*

Antonyms: *calm, appease, pacify, placate*

English Example: *Jason Gillespie advised Australian team not to rile up Virat Kohli.*

Hindi Example: जेसन गिलेस्पी ने ऑस्ट्रेलियाई टीम को सलाह दी कि विराट कोहली को गुस्सा ना दिलाए।

Date: 2017/09/16

WOD: *Evangelist*

Pronunciation: इ-वैन्जलिस्ट

Type of word (Category): *Noun*

English meaning: *a zealous advocate of a particular cause*

Hindi meaning: प्रचारक

Synonyms: *advocate, supporter, promoter, proponent, exponent, campaigner*

Antonyms: -

English Example: *President Kovind urged to Hindi evangelists to respect regional languages.*

Hindi Example: राष्ट्रपति कोविन्द ने हिंदी प्रचारकों से क्षेत्रीय भाषाओं का सम्मान करने का आग्रह किया।

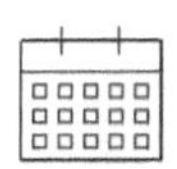 **Date: 2017/09/17**

WOD: *Iota*

Pronunciation: आइ-ओट

Type of word (Category): Noun

English meaning: an extremely small amount

Hindi meaning: तिलमात्र

Synonyms: bit, mite, speck, scrap, jot, tittle

Antonyms: lot, bunch, abundance, bundle

English Example: Kangana Ranaut is more than happy to let go of this industry, because she doesn't have an iota of respect for it.

Hindi Example: कंगना राणावत इस उद्योग को छोड़ देने में बहुत खुश हैं, क्योंकि इसके लिए उसे तिलमात्र का सम्मान नहीं है।

Date: 2017/09/18

WOD: *Melee*

Pronunciation: मेले

Type of word (Category): Noun

English meaning: a confused fight or scuffle

Hindi meaning: हंगामा

Synonyms: tumult, disturbance, rumpus, commotion, disorder, brawl

Antonyms: peace, compromise, agreement

English Example: In the melee, E Palaniswami has marked his arrival in AIADMK party.

Hindi Example: हंगामें में, ई पलानीसामी ने एआईएडीएमके पार्टी में अपने आगमन को चिह्नित किया है।

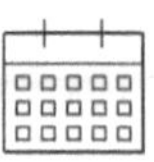 **Date: 2017/09/19**

WOD: *Flamboyance*

Pronunciation: फ़्लेम्बॉइअन्स

Type of word (Category): Noun

English meaning: the tendency to attract attention because of one's exuberance, confidence, and stylishness

Hindi meaning: आकर्षण

Synonyms: showiness, ostentation, gaudiness, opulence

Antonyms: clumsiness, dullness, modesty, ordinariness

English Example: Hardik Pandya's all-round flamboyance helped India to record a comfortable 26-run win over Australia.

Hindi Example: हार्दिक पंड्या के चौतरफा आकर्षण ने भारत को ऑस्ट्रेलिया पर 26 रनों की शानदार जीत दर्ज करने में मदद की।

Date: 2017/09/20

WOD: *Irrigation*

Pronunciation: इरगैशन

Type of word (Category): Noun

English meaning: the supply of water to land or crops to help growth, typically by means of channels

Hindi meaning: सिंचाई

Synonyms: watering, immersion, flushing, douche

Antonyms: drainage

English Example: The Sardar Sarovar dam is expected to provide power, drinking water and irrigation to 9,000 villages in three states.

Hindi Example: सरदार सरोवर बांध से तीन राज्यों में 9,000 गांवों तक बिजली, पेयजल और सिंचाई उपलब्ध कराने की उम्मीद है।

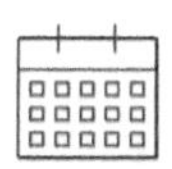 **Date: 2017/09/21**

WOD: *Attire*

Pronunciation: अ-टायर

Type of word (Category):   *Noun*

English meaning: *clothes, especially fine or formal ones*

Hindi meaning: पोशाक

Synonyms: *clothing, garments, dress, costume, array, apparel*

Antonyms: -

English Example: *Garba, a folk dance in a traditional attire, rehearsed ahead of Navratri.*

Hindi Example: गरबा, पारंपरिक पोशाक में एक लोक नृत्य, का नवरात्रि से पहले अभ्यास किया गया।

 **Date: 2017/09/22**

WOD: *Depraved*

Pronunciation: डि-प्रेव्ड

Type of word (Category):   *Adjective*

English meaning: *morally bad or evil*

Hindi meaning: पथभ्रष्ट

Synonyms: *corrupt, deviant, degraded, immoral, unprincipled, dissolute*

Antonyms: *prude, benevolent, ethical, awesome, decent*

English Example: *Rishi Kapoor recently slammed a cartoon on the RK studio fire and called it 'depraved sick humour'.*

Hindi Example: ऋषि कपूर ने हाल ही में आरके स्टूडियो आग पर एक कार्टून की कटु आलोचना की और इसे 'पथभ्रष्ट बीमार हास्य' का नाम दिया।

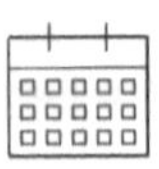 **Date: 2017/09/23**

WOD: *Square*

Pronunciation: स्क्वेर

Type of word (Category): *Verb*

English meaning: *make the score of (a match or game) even, balance (an account)*

Hindi meaning: बराबर करना

Synonyms: *level, even, settle, even up, make equal, balance*

Antonyms: *differ, fail, vary, separate*

English Example: *Kuldeep Yadav's hat-trick snuffed out Australia's hopes of squaring the series.*

Hindi Example: कुलदीप यादव की हेट-ट्रिक ने ऑस्ट्रेलिया की सीरीज़ को बराबर करने की उम्मीदों को बुझा दिया।

Date: 2017/09/24

WOD: *Obstinate*

Pronunciation: ऑब्स्टनट

Type of word (Category): *Adjective*

English meaning: *stubbornly refusing to change one's opinion or chosen course of action, despite attempts to persuade one to do so*

Hindi meaning: ज़िद्दी

Synonyms: *stubborn, headstrong, wilful, unyielding, inflexible, uncompromising*

Antonyms: *flexible, docile, obedient, submissive*

English Example: *Supreme Court expressed anguish over 'obstinate behaviour' of BCCI officials over draft constitution.*

Hindi Example: सुप्रीम कोर्ट ने बीसीसीआई अधिकारियों के प्रारूप संविधान पर 'ज़िद्दी व्यवहार' पर चिंता व्यक्त की।

 **Date: 2017/09/25**

WOD: *Ambit*

Pronunciation: ऐम्बिट

Type of word (Category): Noun

English meaning: the range or limits of the influence of something

Hindi meaning: क्षेत्र

Synonyms: range, circuit, periphery, orbit, purview

Antonyms: -

English Example: Vehicle users shouldn't harbour hopes of petrol and diesel coming under the ambit of GST.

Hindi Example: वाहन उपयोगकर्ताओं को पेट्रोल और डीजल का जीएसटी के क्षेत्र के तहत आने की उम्मीद नहीं करनी चाहिए।

 **Date: 2017/09/26**

WOD: *Unanimous*

Pronunciation: यू-नेनमस

Type of word (Category): Adjective

English meaning: (of two or more people) fully in agreement

Hindi meaning: सर्वसम्मत

Synonyms: united, accordant, harmonious, concordant, concurrent

Antonyms: split, conflicting, diversified, irreconcilable

English Example: The Hindi film 'Newton', India's official entry to Oscars 2018, was the unanimous choice of FFI's selection committee.

Hindi Example: हिंदी फिल्म 'न्यूटन', ऑस्कर 2018 में भारत की आधिकारिक प्रविष्टि, एफएफआई की चयन समिति की सर्वसम्मत पसंद थी।

SEPTEMBER

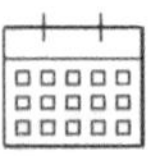

Date: 2017/09/27

WOD: *Unflagging*

Pronunciation:　अन्फ्लैगिंग

Type of word (Category):　Adjective

English meaning:　tireless; persistent

Hindi meaning:　निरंतर

Synonyms:　persistent, tenacious, determined, resolute, staunch

Antonyms:　inconstant, changing, wavering, variable

English Example:　Kamal Haasan has criticised the Tamil Nadu government for corruption and unflagging self-interest.

Hindi Example:　कमल हसन ने तमिलनाडु सरकार की भ्रष्टाचार और निरंतर स्वार्थपरता के लिए आलोचना की।

Date: 2017/09/28

WOD: *Languish*

Pronunciation:　लैंग्विश

Type of word (Category):　Verb

English meaning:　to exist in an unpleasant or unwanted situation, often for a long time

Hindi meaning:　कमजोर होना

Synonyms:　weaken, deteriorate, flag, decline, wither

Antonyms:　recover, improve, flourish, prosper

English Example:　Dabang Delhi is languishing at the bottom of the table in Zone A in the fifth season of VIVO Pro Kabaddi League.

Hindi Example:　दबंग दिल्ली वीवो प्रो कबड्डी लीग के पांचवें सत्र में जोन ए की तालिका में सबसे नीचे कमजोर पड़े हुए हैं।

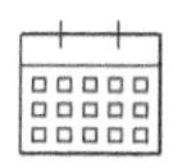 **Date: 2017/09/29**

WOD: *Spellbound*

Pronunciation: स्पेल्बाउन्ड

Type of word (Category): Adjective

English meaning: hold the complete attention of (someone) as though by magic; fascinate

Hindi meaning: मंत्रमुग्ध

Synonyms: fascinated, charmed, enchanted, enraptured, captivated, bewitched

Antonyms: disinterested, disenchanted, bored, inattentive

English Example: Everyone in Kolkata is spellbound by the festive look of the city itself.

Hindi Example: कोलकाता में सभी लोग शहर के उत्सवी रूप से मंत्रमुग्ध है।

Date: 2017/09/30

WOD: *Locale*

Pronunciation: लो-कैल

Type of word (Category): Noun

English meaning: a place where something happens or is set, or that has particular events associated with it

Hindi meaning: स्थान

Synonyms: place, site, location, setting, background, backdrop

Antonyms: -

English Example: The story of Judwaa 2 is almost the same as earlier movie Judwaa, just moved to the international locales of London.

Hindi Example: जुड़वा 2 की कहानी लगभग पहले की फिल्म जुड़वा के समान है, सिर्फ लंदन के अंतरराष्ट्रीय स्थानों में बदल गई है।

October 2017

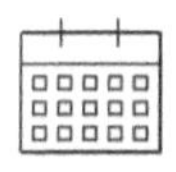 **Date: 2017/10/01**

WOD: *Exodus*

Pronunciation: एक्सडस

Type of word (Category): Noun

English meaning: a mass departure of people

Hindi meaning: पलायन

Synonyms: withdrawal, evacuation, exit, departure, egress

Antonyms: arrival, influx, inflow, entry

English Example: Fears of Bali volcano eruption spark exodus of nearly 100,000 people.

Hindi Example: बाली ज्वालामुखी विस्फोट के डर से लगभग 100,000 लोगों का पलायन।

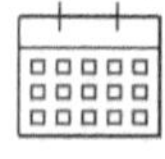 **Date: 2017/10/02**

WOD: *Tycoon*

Pronunciation: टाइ-कून

Type of word (Category): Noun

English meaning: a wealthy, powerful person in business or industry

Hindi meaning: शक्तिशाली उद्योगपति

Synonyms: magnate, baron, industrialist, financier, entrepreneur

Antonyms: pauper, beggar

English Example: Billionaire businessman Sajjan Jindal is the first tycoon to undertake a project cleaning up ghats.

Hindi Example: अरबपति व्यापारी सज्जन जिंदल घाटों की सफाई के लिए शुरू परियोजना का उत्तरदायित्व लेने वाले पहले शक्तिशाली उद्योगपति हैं।

OCTOBER

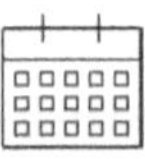 **Date: 2017/10/03**

WOD: *Segregate*

Pronunciation: सेग्रगिट

Type of word (Category):   Verb

English meaning: set apart from the rest or from each other; isolate or divide

Hindi meaning: विभाजित करना

Synonyms: separate, isolate, sequester, dissociate

Antonyms: unite, integrate, combine, desegregate

English Example: Filmmaker Karan Johar said there is need to stop segregating cinema into regions.

Hindi Example: फिल्म निर्माता करण जौहर ने कहा कि सिनेमा को क्षेत्रों में विभाजित करना बंद करने की आवश्यकता है।

Date: 2017/10/04

WOD: *Pioneer*

Pronunciation: पाय-नियर

Type of word (Category):   Verb

English meaning: develop or be the first to use or apply (a new method, area of knowledge, or activity)

Hindi meaning: मार्ग दिखलाना

Synonyms: initiate, develop, instigate, introduce, evolve, institute

Antonyms: close (down), finish, halt, wind up

English Example: The year's first Nobel went to three Americans who pioneered the study of the biological clock.

Hindi Example: साल का पहला नोबेल तीन अमेरिकियों के पास गया, जिन्होंने जैविक घड़ी (बॉयलोजिकल क्लॉक) के अध्ययन का मार्ग दिखलाया।

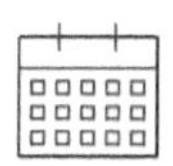

Date: 2017/10/05

WOD: *Buckle*

Pronunciation: बकल

Type of word (Category): *Verb*

English meaning: *bend and give way under pressure or strain*

Hindi meaning: झुकना

Synonyms: *bend, bow, sink, diverge, bevel*

Antonyms: *inflate, rise*

English Example: *Govt buckled to public pressure, cut excise duty on petrol and diesel by Rs. 2 per litre.*

Hindi Example: सरकार जनता के दबाव के आगे झुकी, पेट्रोल और डीजल पर उत्पाद शुल्क में 2 रुपये प्रति लीटर की कटौती की।

OCTOBER

Date: 2017/10/06

WOD: *Tenure*

Pronunciation: टेन्यर

Type of word (Category): *Noun*

English meaning: *the right to remain permanently in a job*

Hindi meaning: कार्यकाल

Synonyms: *possession, occupancy, incumbency, tenancy, hold*

Antonyms: -

English Example: *Rajnish Kumar's appointment as the next chairman of SBI has been made for a tenure of three years.*

Hindi Example: एसबीआई के अगले अध्यक्ष के रूप में रजनीश कुमार की नियुक्ति तीन साल के कार्यकाल के लिए की गई है।

 **Date: 2017/10/07**

WOD: *Affable*

Pronunciation: ऐफ़बल

Type of word (Category): Adjective

English meaning: friendly, good-natured, or easy to talk to

Hindi meaning: मिलनसार

Synonyms: friendly, amiable, genial, congenial, cordial, pleasant

Antonyms: unfriendly, grouchy, harsh, unsociable

English Example: Saif Ali Khan's Chef is a light and affable film.

Hindi Example: सैफ अली खान की शेफ एक हल्की और मिलनसार फिल्म है।

Date: 2017/10/08

WOD: *Watershed*

Pronunciation: वॉटर्शेड

Type of word (Category): Noun

English meaning: an event or period marking a turning point in a situation

Hindi meaning: ऐतिहासिक घटना

Synonyms: landmark, turning point, milepost, milestone

Antonyms: -

English Example: Organizing FIFA U-17 World Cup is a watershed moment for Indian football.

Hindi Example: फीफा अंडर -17 विश्व कप का आयोजन भारतीय फुटबॉल के लिए एक ऐतिहासिक घटना है।

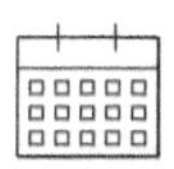

Date: 2017/10/09

WOD: *Lackluster*

Pronunciation: लैक्लस्टर

Type of word (Category):   Adjective

English meaning: lacking in vitality, force, or conviction; uninspired or uninspiring

Hindi meaning: फीका

Synonyms: dull, drab, lustreless, dismal, vapid

Antonyms: bright, lively, playful, revitalizing

English Example: Suresh Raina is out of Team India because of his lackluster form and fitness.

Hindi Example: सुरेश रैना अपने फीके फॉर्म और फिटनेस के कारण टीम इंडिया से बाहर हैं।

Date: 2017/10/10

WOD: *Reliance*

Pronunciation: रि-लाइअन्स

Type of word (Category):   Noun

English meaning: dependence on or trust in someone or something

Hindi meaning: भरोसा

Synonyms: dependence, dependency, confidence, assuredness, trust

Antonyms: doubt, disbelief, distrust, autonomy

English Example: India is planning to lessen its pharmaceutical products' reliance on China.

Hindi Example: भारत चीन पर अपने फ़ार्मासूटिकल उत्पादों के भरोसे को कम करने की योजना बना रहा है।

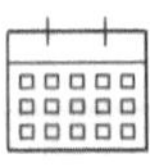 **Date: 2017/10/11**

WOD: *Rung*

Pronunciation: रंग

Type of word (Category): Noun

English meaning: any of the short bars that form the steps of a ladder

Hindi meaning: पायदान

Synonyms: step, point, level, notch, degree

Antonyms: -

English Example: Colombia may be many rungs above India, but India got the momentum by scoring first ever goal in FIFA World Cup.

Hindi Example: कोलम्बिया भारत से कई पायदान आगे हो सकता है, लेकिन फीफा विश्व कप में भारत को पहला गोल करने के बाद गति मिली।

Date: 2017/10/12

WOD: *Revered*

Pronunciation: रिविर्ड

Type of word (Category): Adjective

English meaning: profoundly honored

Hindi meaning: श्रद्धेय

Synonyms: respected, venerable, esteemed, adored, venerated

Antonyms: dishonorable, disreputable, dishonored, despised

English Example: For the revered Amitabh Bachchan, the team of KBC 9 created a video from Sherwood College, Nainital, to celebrate his birthday.

Hindi Example: श्रद्धेय अमिताभ बच्चन के लिए, केबीसी 9 की टीम ने उनके जन्मदिन का जश्न मनाने के लिए शेरवुड कॉलेज, नैनीताल से एक वीडियो बनाया।

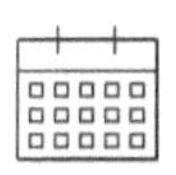 **Date: 2017/10/13**

WOD: *Maul*

Pronunciation: मॉःल

Type of word (Category): *Verb*

English meaning: *defeat heavily in a game or match*

Hindi meaning: आसानी से पराजित कर देना

Synonyms: *batter, beat, thrash, defeat, crush*

Antonyms: *protect, guard, help, assist*

English Example: *India mauled Japan 5-1 in Asia Cup Hockey opening match.*

Hindi Example: एशिया कप हॉकी उद्घाटन मैच में भारत ने जापान को 5-1 से आसानी से पराजित कर दिया।

 **Date: 2017/10/14**

WOD: *Emulate*

Pronunciation: एम्यूलेट

Type of word (Category): *Verb*

English meaning: *match or surpass (a person or achievement), typically by imitation*

Hindi meaning: बराबरी करना

Synonyms: *imitate, reproduce, echo, match, parallel, approximate*

Antonyms: *neglect, reject, overlook, dispossess*

English Example: *According to Shikhar Dhawan if Indian team will emulate Waugh's Australian team, it would be great.*

Hindi Example: शिखर धवन के मुताबिक यदि भारतीय टीम वॉ की ऑस्ट्रेलियाई टीम की बराबरी करती है, तो यह बहुत अच्छा होगा।

OCTOBER

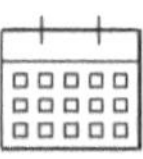 **Date: 2017/10/15**

WOD: *Secede*

Pronunciation: सि-सीड

Type of word (Category):   *Verb*

English meaning: *withdraw formally from membership of a federal union, an alliance, or a political or religious organization*

Hindi meaning: अलग हो जाना

Synonyms: *withdraw, leave, break away, separate, quit*

Antonyms: *combine, join, come together, unite*

English Example: *Many people rallied in Barcelona to protest against the plans of Catalonia's regional government to secede from Spain.*

Hindi Example: बहुत से लोगों ने स्पेन से अलग हो जाने के कैटलोनिया की क्षेत्रीय सरकार की योजनाओं के विरोध में बार्सिलोना में विरोध किया।

Date: 2017/10/16

WOD: *Menacing*

Pronunciation: मेनसिंग

Type of word (Category):   *Verb*

English meaning: *suggesting the presence of danger; threatening*

Hindi meaning: डरावना

Synonyms: *sinister, threatening, forbidding, dangerous, threatening*

Antonyms: *harmless, acceptable, safe, good*

English Example: *Ranveer Singh as ruthless and menacing Allaudin Khilji in Padmavati left all with racing hearts.*

Hindi Example: पद्मावती में रणवीर सिंह ने क्रूर और डरावने अलाउदीन खिलजी के रूप में सभी को धड़कते दिलों के साथ छोड़ा।

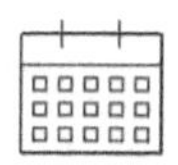

Date: 2017/10/17

WOD: *Amass*

Pronunciation: अ-मस

Type of word (Category): Verb

English meaning: gather together or accumulate (a large amount or number of material or things) over a period of time

Hindi meaning: इकट्ठा करना

Synonyms: gather, collect, assemble, accumulate, hoard

Antonyms: disperse, divide, dissipate, scatter

English Example: Chinese President Xi Jinping is set to amass greater power at a Communist Party Congress.

Hindi Example: चीनी राष्ट्रपति शी जिनपिंग कम्युनिस्ट पार्टी महासभा में अधिक शक्तियां इकट्ठा करने के लिए तैयार हैं।

Date: 2017/10/18

WOD: *Brisk*

Pronunciation: ब्रिस्क

Type of word (Category): Verb

English meaning: active and energetic

Hindi meaning: तेज़

Synonyms: quick, rapid, fast, swift, speedy

Antonyms: sluggish, slow, quiet, lethargic

English Example: Earthen lamp vendors are making brisk business after cracker ban.

Hindi Example: मिट्टी के दीपक विक्रेता पटाखों पर प्रतिबंध के बाद तेज़ कारोबार कर रहे हैं।

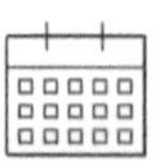 **Date: 2017/10/19**

WOD: *Cacophony*

Pronunciation: के-कॉफ़नी

Type of word (Category):   Noun

English meaning: *a harsh discordant mixture of sounds*

Hindi meaning: कोलाहल

Synonyms: *discord, noise, chaos, dissonance, harshness*

Antonyms: *silence, calm, serenity, quiet*

English Example: *It will be cacophony and smoke free Diwali this year in Delhi NCR as SC banned the sale of firecrackers.*

Hindi Example: दिल्ली एनसीआर में इस साल कोलाहल और धुआं मुक्त दीवाली होगी क्योंकि सुप्रीम कोर्ट ने पटाखों की बिक्री पर प्रतिबंध लगा दिया है।

Date: 2017/10/20

WOD: *Pinnacle*

Pronunciation: पिनॅकॅल

Type of word (Category):   Noun

English meaning: *the most successful point; the culmination*

Hindi meaning: शिखर

Synonyms: *highest level, peak, zenith, acme, summit*

Antonyms: *base, bottom, nadir, basis*

English Example: *Some parts of Secret Superstar touch the pinnacle of the storytelling.*

Hindi Example: सीक्रेट सुपरस्टार के कुछ हिस्से कहानी कहने की कला के शिखर को छूते हैं।

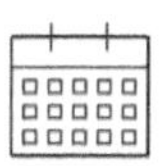

Date: 2017/10/21

WOD: *Setback*

Pronunciation: सेट्बैक

Type of word (Category): Noun

English meaning: *a reversal or check in progress*

Hindi meaning: बाधा

Synonyms: *problem, difficulty, issue, complication, misfortune, mishap*

Antonyms: *blessing, advance, success, triumph*

English Example: *A major setback for S Sreesanth, the Kerala High Court decided to restore the life ban imposed on the bowler by the BCCI.*

Hindi Example: एस श्रीसंत के लिए एक बड़ी बाधा, केरल उच्च न्यायालय ने बीसीसीआई द्वारा गेंदबाज पर लगाए गए आजीवन प्रतिबंध को पुनर्स्थापित करने का निर्णय लिया।

Date: 2017/10/22

WOD: *Condense*

Pronunciation: कन्डेन्स

Type of word (Category): Verb

English meaning: *express (written or spoken material) in fewer words; make concise*

Hindi meaning: संक्षिप्त करना

Synonyms: *abridge, shorten, compress, compact, summarize*

Antonyms: *expand, enlarge, amplify, extend*

English Example: *Tendulkar's autobiography 'Playing It My Way' is being condensed with a section of it projecting Tendulkar as a comic book hero.*

Hindi Example: तेंदुलकर की आत्मकथा 'प्लेइंग इट माय वे' के एक खंड को संक्षिप्त किया जा रहा है जिसमें तेंदुलकर को हास्य पुस्तक के नायक के रूप में पेश किया जा रहा है।

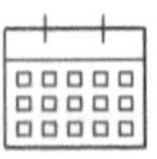 **Date: 2017/10/23**

WOD: *Reduction*

Pronunciation: रि-डॅक्शन

Type of word (Category): Noun

English meaning: the action or fact of making something smaller or less in amount, degree, or size

Hindi meaning: कटौती

Synonyms: decrease, lessening, diminution, deduction

Antonyms: increase, surge, addition, increment

English Example: There is a possibility to back a reduction in the levy on restaurants from 18% to 12% by GST Council.

Hindi Example: जीएसटी कॉउन्सिल द्वारा रेस्तरां में आरोपित राशि में 18% से 12% तक की कटौती का समर्थन करने की संभावना है।

Date: 2017/10/24

WOD: *Gutsy*

Pronunciation: गट्सी

Type of word (Category): Adjective

English meaning: having or showing courage, determination, and spirit

Hindi meaning: जोशीला

Synonyms: courageous, daring, mettlesome, brave, valorous, intrepid

Antonyms: coward, shy, timid, gutless

English Example: India beat a gutsy Malaysia 2-1 in a nail-biting final to clinch their third Asia Cup hockey title.

Hindi Example: भारत ने अपना तीसरा एशिया कप हॉकी का खिताब जीतने के लिए एक बहुत ही रोमांचक फाइनल में जोशीले मलेशिया को 2-1 से हराया।

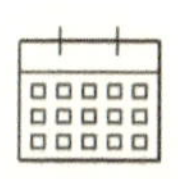

Date: 2017/10/25

WOD: *Interlocutor*

Pronunciation: इन्टर्लाक्यिटर

Type of word (Category): Noun

English meaning: a person who takes part in a dialogue or conversation

Hindi meaning: वार्ताकार

Synonyms: speaker, conversational partner, conversationalist, talker, interrogator

Antonyms: -

English Example: Government appointed former IB Director Dineshwar Sharma as special interlocutor on Kashmir.

Hindi Example: सरकार ने आईबी के पूर्व निदेशक दिनेश्वर शर्मा को कश्मीर पर विशेष वार्ताकार के रूप में नियुक्त किया।

Date: 2017/10/26

WOD: *Manoeuvre*

Pronunciation: मॅ-नूवॅं

Type of word (Category): Noun

English meaning: a movement or series of moves requiring skill and care

Hindi meaning: कौशल

Synonyms: trick, stratagem, ruse, move, tactic

Antonyms: -

English Example: India Air Force planes displayed breathtaking manoeuvres before landing on the Lucknow-Agra Expressway.

Hindi Example: लखनऊ-आगरा एक्सप्रेसवे पर उतरने से पहले भारतीय वायु सेना के विमानों ने विस्मयकारी कौशल दिखाए।

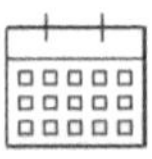 **Date: 2017/10/27**

WOD: *Clinical*

Pronunciation: क्लिनिकल

Type of word (Category): Adjective

English meaning: *very efficient and without feeling; coldly detached*

Hindi meaning: भावशून्य

Synonyms: *rational, logical, detached, impersonal, hard-headed*

Antonyms: *subjective, theoretical, passionate*

English Example: *India produced a clinical performance under pressure to beat New Zealand by six wickets.*

Hindi Example: भारत ने दबाव में एक भावशून्य प्रदर्शन करते हुए न्यूजीलैंड को छह विकेट से हरा दिया।

 **Date: 2017/10/28**

WOD: *Grandiose*

Pronunciation: ग्रेन्डीअस

Type of word (Category): Adjective

English meaning: extravagantly or pretentiously imposing in appearance or style

Hindi meaning: भव्यता

Synonyms: *magnificent, impressive, grand, imposing, resplendent*

Antonyms: *unimpressive, unpretentious, moderate, modest*

English Example: *Sanjay Leela Bhansali's vision can be seen in the grandiose of the set of Padmavati.*

Hindi Example: संजय लीला भंसाली की दूरदर्शिता पद्मावती के सेट की भव्यता में देखी जा सकती है।

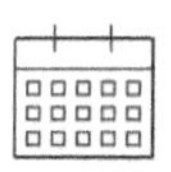

Date: 2017/10/29

WOD: *Horizon*

Pronunciation: ह-राइज़न

Type of word (Category): Noun

English meaning: the limit of a person's knowledge, experience, or interest

Hindi meaning: क्षितिज

Synonyms: outlook, perspective, perception, compass, sphere, ambit, orbit, purview

Antonyms: -

English Example: According to Van Basten, football in India will get a new horizon with the U-17 World Cup.

Hindi Example: वान बास्टेन के अनुसार, भारत में फुटबॉल को अंडर -17 विश्व कप के साथ एक नया क्षितिज मिलेगा।

Date: 2017/10/30

WOD: *Twirl*

Pronunciation: ट्वर्ल

Type of word (Category): Noun

English meaning: an act of spinning

Hindi meaning: घुमाव

Synonyms: spin, whirl, twist, gyrate, swirl

Antonyms: -

English Example: Deepika reportedly performed over 66 twirls for the song 'Ghoomar'.

Hindi Example: खबरों के अनुसार दीपिका ने 'घूमर' गीत के लिए 66 से अधिक घुमावों का प्रदर्शन किया।

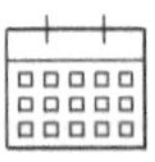 **Date: 2017/10/31**

WOD: *Dent*

Pronunciation: डेन्ट

Type of word (Category): *Verb*

English meaning: *have an adverse effect on, diminish*

Hindi meaning: क्षति पहुंचना

Synonyms: *diminish, reduce, destroy, damage, crush*

Antonyms: *boost, gain, increase*

English Example: *Bumrah and Chahal gave timely dent to Kiwis' batting in 3rd ODI.*

Hindi Example: बुमराह और चहल ने तीसरे एकदिवसी मैच में न्यूजीलैंड की बल्लेबाजी को ठीक समय पर क्षति पहुंचाई।

November 2017

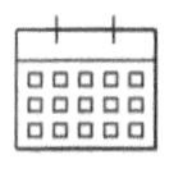

Date: 2017/11/01

WOD: *Monumental*

Pronunciation: मान्यू-मेन्टल

Type of word (Category): Adjective

English meaning: great in importance, extent, or size

Hindi meaning: महत्वपूर्ण

Synonyms: valuable, important, meaningful

Antonyms: little, insignificant, unimportant, small

English Example: PM Modi remembered Sardar Patel's monumental contribution to India on Sardar Patel's birth anniversary.

Hindi Example: सरदार पटेल की जयंती पर प्रधान मंत्री मोदी ने भारत में सरदार पटेल के महत्वपूर्ण योगदान को याद किया।

Date: 2017/11/02

WOD: *Epidemic*

Pronunciation: एपि-डेमिक

Type of word (Category): Noun

English meaning: a widespread occurrence of an infectious disease in a community at a particular time

Hindi meaning: महामारी

Synonyms: plague, outbreak, pandemic, pestilence

Antonyms: -

English Example: Experts are worried as new dengue virus is linked to severe and extensive epidemics in India and abroad.

Hindi Example: विशेषज्ञों को चिंता है कि नया डेंगू वायरस भारत और विदेशों में गंभीर और व्यापक महामारियों से जुड़ा हुआ है।

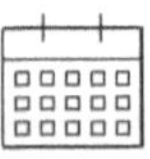 **Date: 2017/11/03**

WOD: *Sturdy*

Pronunciation: स्टर्डी

Type of word (Category): Adjective

English meaning: showing confidence and determination

Hindi meaning: दृढ़

Synonyms: vigorous, firm, determined, resolute, unwavering

Antonyms: unstable, weak, feeble, frail

English Example: Ashish Nehra's sturdy resolve is difficult to match.

Hindi Example: आशिष नेहरा के दृढ़ निश्चय का मेल करना कठिन है।

Date: 2017/11/04

WOD: *Demarcate*

Pronunciation: डीमाकेट

Type of word (Category): Verb

English meaning: set the boundaries or limits of

Hindi meaning: निर्धारित करना

Synonyms: delimit, define, circumscribe, bound, limit

Antonyms: combine, connect

English Example: Delhi government approached the SC to demarcate the powers between the Centre and the Delhi government.

Hindi Example: दिल्ली सरकार ने केंद्र और दिल्ली सरकार के बीच की शक्तियों को निर्धारित करने के लिए सुप्रीम कोर्ट से संपर्क किया।

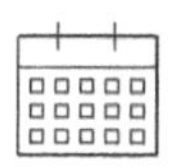 **Date: 2017/11/05**

WOD: *Hazard*

Pronunciation: हैज़र्ड

Type of word (Category): Noun

English meaning: *a danger or risk*

Hindi meaning: खतरा

Synonyms: *danger, risk, peril, threat, menace*

Antonyms: *safety, safeguard, protect, protection*

English Example: *Early morning walks for Delhiites can cause to severe health hazards due to the city's toxic air.*

Hindi Example: शहर की जहरीली हवा के कारण सुबह की सैर दिल्लीवासियों के लिए गंभीर स्वास्थ्य खतरा पैदा कर सकती है।

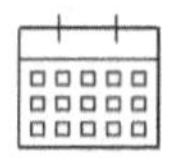 **Date: 2017/11/06**

WOD: *Whodunit*

Pronunciation: हू-डनिट

Type of word (Category): Noun

English meaning: *a story or play about a murder in which the identity of the murderer is not revealed until the end*

Hindi meaning: जासूसी कहानी

Synonyms: *mystery, riddle, enigma, conundrum*

Antonyms: -

English Example: *Sidharth Malhotra-Sonakshi Sinha starrer film 'Ittefaq' is a gritty whodunit.*

Hindi Example: सिद्धार्थ मल्होत्रा-सोनाक्षी सिन्हा की फिल्म 'इत्तेफाक' एक दृढ़ जासूसी कहानी है।

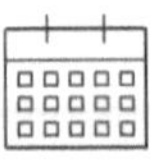 **Date: 2017/11/07**

WOD: *Sheer*

Pronunciation: शिअ

Type of word (Category): Adjective

English meaning: nothing other than; unmitigated (used for emphasis)

Hindi meaning: पूर्णतया

Synonyms: utter, complete, absolute, total, pure, unmitigated

Antonyms: incomplete, moderate, uncertain, impure

English Example: India women's hockey team won Asia Cup 2017 with sheer dominance.

Hindi Example: भारत की महिला हॉकी टीम ने पूर्णतया प्रभुत्व के साथ एशिया कप 2017 जीता।

Date: 2017/11/08

WOD: *Horde*

Pronunciation: हॉर्ड

Type of word (Category): Noun

English meaning: a large group of people

Hindi meaning: भीड़

Synonyms: crowd, swarm, throng, group, bunch

Antonyms: little, portion, bit

English Example: In India, all major metros witnessed hordes of people lining up at Apple stores to get iPhone X.

Hindi Example: भारत में, सभी प्रमुख महानगरों ने एप्पल स्टोरों में आईफोन X लेने के लिए लोगों की भीड़ को कतारों में लगे देखा।

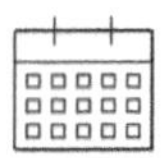

Date: 2017/11/09

WOD: *Haze*

Pronunciation: हेज़

Type of word (Category):   Noun

English meaning: a slight obscuration of the lower atmosphere, typically caused by fine suspended particles

Hindi meaning: धुंध

Synonyms: mist, fog, cloud, smog, gauze

Antonyms: clarity, cleanness, clearness

English Example: Delhi is shrouded again in a toxic grey haze.

Hindi Example: दिल्ली एक बार फिर से जहरीले भूरे धुंध में छिप गई है।

Date: 2017/11/10

WOD: *Indomitable*

Pronunciation: इन्डामिटबल

Type of word (Category):   Adjective

English meaning: impossible to subdue or defeat

Hindi meaning: अजय

Synonyms: invincible, unconquerable, unbeatable, unassailable, unsurpassable

Antonyms: conquerable, weak, submissive, powerless

English Example: Every medal is a story of struggle, said the indomitable Mary Kom after winning gold medal in Asian Boxing Championship.

Hindi Example: हर पदक संघर्ष की एक कहानी है, अजय मैरी कॉम ने एशियाई मुक्केबाजी चैंपियनशिप में स्वर्ण पदक जीतने के बाद कहा।

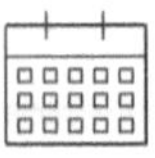 **Date: 2017/11/11**

WOD: *Ouster*

Pronunciation: आउस्टर

Type of word (Category):   Noun

English meaning: the process of removing someone from an important position or job

Hindi meaning: निकाल देना

Synonyms: expulsion, removal, eviction, dismissal, overthrow

Antonyms: welcoming, hiring

English Example: Several former cricketers called for Dhoni's T20 ouster.

Hindi Example: कई पूर्व क्रिकेटरों ने धोनी को टी20 से निकाल देने की मांग की।

Date: 2017/11/12

WOD: *Enforce*

Pronunciation: इन्फ़ॉर्स

Type of word (Category):   Verb

English meaning: compel observance of or compliance with (a law, rule, or obligation)

Hindi meaning: लागू करना

Synonyms: force, implement, impose, compel, apply

Antonyms: neglect, exempt, relieve, free

English Example: The odd-even scheme will be enforced in Delhi for a period of five days to tackle the deteriorating air quality in the national capital.

Hindi Example: राष्ट्रीय राजधानी में बिगड़ती हुई हवा की गुणवत्ता से निपटने के लिए पांच दिनों की समयावधि के लिए ऑड-ईवन योजना को दिल्ली में लागू किया जाएगा।

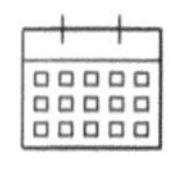 **Date: 2017/11/13**

WOD: *Noteworthy*

Pronunciation: नोट्वर्दी

Type of word (Category): *Adjective*

English meaning: *worth paying attention to; interesting or significant*

Hindi meaning: उल्लेखनीय

Synonyms: *notable, outstanding, remarkable, noticeable, significant*

Antonyms: *insignificant, ordinary, average, unimportant*

English Example: *Rajkummar Rao has delivered another noteworthy performance in 'Shaadi Mein Zaroor Aana' movie.*

Hindi Example: राजकुमार राव ने 'शादी में ज़रूर आना' फिल्म में एक और उल्लेखनीय प्रदर्शन दिया है।

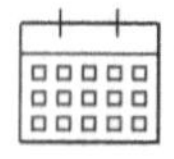 **Date: 2017/11/14**

WOD: *Quash*

Pronunciation: क्वॉश

Type of word (Category): *Verb*

English meaning: *reject as invalid, especially by legal procedure*

Hindi meaning: अमान्य घोषित करना

Synonyms: *invalidate, nullify, subdue, cancel, negate, void*

Antonyms: *validate, enforce, sanction, uphold*

English Example: *Supreme Court quashed plea to ban Padmavati.*

Hindi Example: सुप्रीम कोर्ट ने पदमावती पर प्रतिबंध लगाने की याचिका को अमान्य घोषित किया।

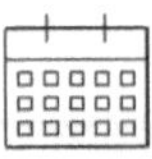 **Date: 2017/11/15**

WOD: *Mediocre*

Pronunciation: मीडी-ओकर

Type of word (Category):   Adjective

English meaning: of only average quality; not very good

Hindi meaning: औसत दर्जे का

Synonyms: average, ordinary, common, passable, indifferent

Antonyms: extraordinary, exceptional, excellent, superb

English Example: Italy failed to reach World Cup for first time in 60 years due to their mediocre performance.

Hindi Example: इटली अपने औसत दर्जे के प्रदर्शन के कारण 60 वर्षों में पहली बार विश्व कप तक पहुंचने में असफल रहा।

Date: 2017/11/16

WOD: *Enhance*

Pronunciation: इन्हान्स

Type of word (Category):   Verb

English meaning: to improve its value, quality, or attractiveness

Hindi meaning: बढ़ाना

Synonyms: increase, intensify, magnify, amplify, raise

Antonyms: decrease, diminish, reduce, damage

English Example: According to a new study, regular exercise may help in enhancing your memory.

Hindi Example: एक नए अध्ययन के अनुसार, नियमित व्यायाम आपकी स्मृति को बढ़ाने में मदद कर सकता है।

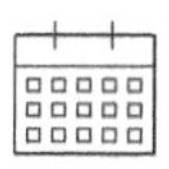

Date: 2017/11/17

WOD: *Cripple*

Pronunciation: क्रिपल

Type of word (Category):   *Verb*

English meaning: *to cause serious damage to someone or something, making him, her, or it weak and not effective*

Hindi meaning: निर्बल करना

Synonyms: *disable, weaken, incapacitate, debilitate, undermine*

Antonyms: *strengthen, enable, encourage, capacitate*

English Example: *Delhi will run on BS-VI grade petrol and diesel from April 1 next year as air pollution has crippled the national capital.*

Hindi Example: दिल्ली अगले साल 1 अप्रैल से बीएस-6 ग्रेड के पेट्रोल और डीजल पर चलेगी क्योंकि वायु प्रदूषण ने राष्ट्रीय राजधानी को निर्बल कर दिया है।

Date: 2017/11/18

WOD: *Timbre*

Pronunciation: टैम्बॅ

Type of word (Category):   *Noun*

English meaning: *the character or quality of a musical sound or voice as distinct from its pitch and intensity*

Hindi meaning: स्वर विशेषता

Synonyms: *tone, resonance, quality, pitch*

Antonyms: *slackness*

English Example: *Vidya Balan's voice has a rich timbre that presents immense possibilities in 'Tumhari Sulu'.*

Hindi Example: विद्या बालन की आवाज़ में एक स्वर विशेषता है जो 'तुम्हारी सुलू' में विशाल संभावनाओं को प्रस्तुत करती है।

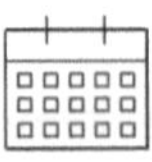 **Date: 2017/11/19**

WOD: *Upgrade*

Pronunciation: अपग्रेड

Type of word (Category): *Verb*

English meaning: raise (something) to a higher standard, give a promotion to or assign to a higher position

Hindi meaning: सुधार करना

Synonyms: elevate, advance, improve, raise, enhance

Antonyms: downgrade, descent, degrade, demote

English Example: Global Rating agency Moody's has upgraded India's local and foreign currency issuer ratings to Baa2 from Baa3.

Hindi Example: ग्लोबल रेटिंग एजेंसी मूडीज ने भारत की स्थानीय और विदेशी मुद्रा जारीकर्ता रेटिंग्स में Baa3 से Baa2 तक सुधार किया है।

Date: 2017/11/20

WOD: *Sacrosanct*

Pronunciation: सेक्रोसेंक्ट

Type of word (Category): *Noun*

English meaning: (especially of a principle, place, or routine) regarded as too important or valuable to be interfered with

Hindi meaning: पवित्र

Synonyms: sacred, blessed, holy, sanctified, inviolable, sanctified

Antonyms: irreligious, unspiritual, earthly

English Example: Right to freedom of speech and expression is sacrosanct and should not be ordinarily interfered with.

Hindi Example: भाषण और अभिव्यक्ति की स्वतंत्रता का अधिकार पवित्र है और इसमें सामान्य रूप से हस्तक्षेप नहीं किया जाना चाहिए।

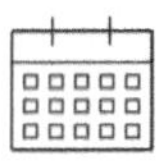 **Date: 2017/11/21**

WOD: *Coveted*

Pronunciation: कवटिंड

Type of word (Category): Adjective

English meaning: strongly desired by many

Hindi meaning: आकांक्षित

Synonyms: desired, wanted, desirable, yearned, in demand

Antonyms: undesirable, disagreeable, detestable, disagreeable

English Example: India's Manushi Chhillar won the coveted 'Miss World 2017' title.

Hindi Example: भारत की मानुषी छिल्लर ने आकांक्षित 'मिस वर्ल्ड 2017' का खिताब जीता।

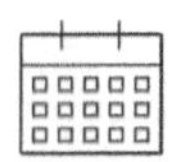 **Date: 2017/11/22**

WOD: *Impeachment*

Pronunciation: इम्पीचमन्ट

Type of word (Category): Noun

English meaning: the action of calling into question the integrity or validity of something, charge of wrongdoing

Hindi meaning: महाभियोग

Synonyms: indictment, accusation, charge, imputation, allegation

Antonyms: approval, commendation, praise, compliment

English Example: Zimbabwe's President Robert Mugabe is going to face impeachment.

Hindi Example: जिम्बाब्वे के राष्ट्रपति रॉबर्ट मुगाबे महाभियोग का सामना करने जा रहे हैं।

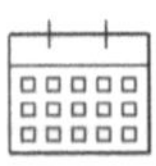 **Date: 2017/11/23**

WOD: *Assiduous*

Pronunciation: अ-सिज़ूअस

Type of word (Category):   Adjective

English meaning: showing hard work, care, and attention to detail

Hindi meaning: परिश्रमयुक्त

Synonyms: diligent, careful, meticulous, industrious, laborious, conscientious

Antonyms: idle, negligent, careless, inert

English Example: India's Dalveer Bhandari re-election in ICJ is probably the most assiduous diplomatic success in recent times.

Hindi Example: आईसीजे में दलवीर भंडारी का पुनर्निर्वाचन संभवत: हाल के दिनों में भारत की सबसे अधिक परिश्रमयुक्त कूटनीतिक सफलता है।

Date: 2017/11/24

WOD: *Arsenal*

Pronunciation: आर्सनल

Type of word (Category):   Noun

English meaning: a place where weapons and military equipment are stored or made

Hindi meaning: शस्त्रागार

Synonyms: armoury, arms depot, ordnance depot, storehouse, ammunition dump

Antonyms: -

English Example: BrahMos missile is the latest addition to India's arsenal which is capable of being launched from land, air and sea.

Hindi Example: ब्रह्मोस मिसाइल भारत के शस्त्रागार में नया संकलन है जो भूमि, वायु और समुद्र से प्रक्षेपित करने में सक्षम है।

 **Date: 2017/11/25**

WOD: *Chide*

Pronunciation: चाइड

Type of word (Category): Verb

English meaning: to speak to someone severely because they have behaved badly

Hindi meaning: डांटना

Synonyms: scold, lambaste, rebuke, reprimand, chastise, upbraid

Antonyms: praise, compliment, laud, applaud

English Example: The Mumbai police chided the actor Varun Dhawan for violating traffic rules.

Hindi Example: ट्रैफिक नियमों का उल्लंघन करने के लिए मुंबई पुलिस ने अभिनेता वरुण धवन को डांटा।

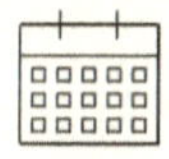 **Date: 2017/11/26**

WOD: *Cramped*

Pronunciation: क्रैम्प्ड

Type of word (Category): Adjective

English meaning: not having enough space or time, uncomfortably small or restricted

Hindi meaning: तंग

Synonyms: tight, close, confined, restricted, limited, compressed

Antonyms: ample, comfortable

English Example: Virat Kohli slammed cramped schedule ahead of South Africa tour.

Hindi Example: दक्षिण अफ्रीका के दौरे से पहले विराट कोहली ने तंग कार्यक्रम की कड़ी आलोचना की।

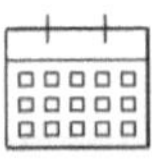 **Date: 2017/11/27**

WOD: *Inconsequential*

Pronunciation: इंगकान्सक्वेन्चल

Type of word (Category): *Adjective*

English meaning: *not important or significant*

Hindi meaning: महत्त्वहीन

Synonyms: *insignificant, unimportant, negligible, petty, trifling*

Antonyms: *important, significant, consequential, essential*

English Example: *Bhaag Bakool Bhaag actor Jay Soni doesn't want to play inconsequential characters in Bollywood.*

Hindi Example: भाग बकुल भाग अभिनेता जय सोनी बॉलीवुड में महत्त्वहीन किरदारों को नहीं निभाना चाहते।

Date: 2017/11/28

WOD: *Stamp*

Pronunciation: स्टैम्प

Type of word (Category): *Verb*

English meaning: *reveal or mark out as having a particular quality or ability*

Hindi meaning: अंकित करना

Synonyms: *identify, characterize, mark out, engrave*

Antonyms: *disallowance, declination*

English Example: *Virat Kohli is stamping his supremacy as a batsman.*

Hindi Example: विराट कोहली एक बल्लेबाज के रूप में अपनी सर्वोच्चता अंकित कर रहे हैं।

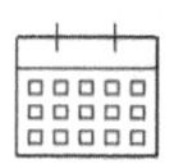

Date: 2017/11/29

WOD: *Thrive*

Pronunciation: थ्राइव

Type of word (Category): *Verb*

English meaning: *to grow, develop, or be successful*

Hindi meaning: कामयाब होना

Synonyms: *succeed, prosper, grow, develop, progress*

Antonyms: *struggle, fail, decline, deteriorate*

English Example: *Ivanka Trump said that no country can thrive without giving equal opportunity to half of its population.*

Hindi Example: इवांका ट्रम्प ने कहा कि कोई भी देश अपनी आधी आबादी को समान अवसर दिए बिना कामयाब नहीं हो सकता।

Date: 2017/11/30

WOD: *Testimony*

Pronunciation: टेस्टमोनी

Type of word (Category): *Noun*

English meaning: *evidence or proof of something*

Hindi meaning: प्रमाण

Synonyms: *testament, proof, evidence, attestation, manifestation*

Antonyms: *disproof, refutation, denial*

English Example: *Muralitharan feels R Ashwin is presently the best spinner and his achievements with the ball are a testimony to his greatness.*

Hindi Example: मुरलीधरन का मानना है कि आर अश्विन वर्तमान में सर्वश्रेष्ठ स्पिनर हैं और गेंद से उनकी उपलब्धियां उनकी महानता का प्रमाण है।

December 2017

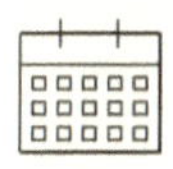

Date: 2017/12/01

WOD: *Surreptitiously*

Pronunciation: सरेप्टि-शस्ली

Type of word (Category):   Adverb

English meaning: in a way that attempts to avoid notice or attention; secretively

Hindi meaning: चुपके से

Synonyms: secretly, furtively, privately, stealthily, covertly

Antonyms: publicly, clearly, openly, directly

English Example: UIDAI has ordered probe against Bharti Airtel for allegedly opening Airtel Payments Bank accounts of customers surreptitiously.

Hindi Example: यूआईडीएआई ने भारती एयरटेल के खिलाफ कथित तौर पर चुपके से ग्राहकों के एयरटेल पेमेंट बैंक खातों को खोलने के खिलाफ जांच के आदेश दिए है।

Date: 2017/12/02

WOD: *Exorcise*

Pronunciation: एक्सॉर्साइज़

Type of word (Category):   Verb

English meaning: completely remove (something unpleasant) from one's mind or memory

Hindi meaning: भूत भगाना

Synonyms: drive out, cast out, expel, purge

Antonyms: welcome, maintain, hold

English Example: Mirabai Chanu exorcised the ghosts of her loss in Rio Olympics by winning the gold medal at the World Weightlifting Championship.

Hindi Example: मीराबाई चानू ने वर्ल्ड वेटलिफ्टिंग चैंपियनशिप में स्वर्ण पदक जीतकर रियो ओलंपिक में अपनी हार के भूत को भगा दिया।

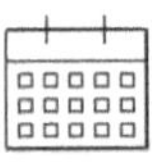

WOD: *Scintillating*

Pronunciation: सिंटीलैटिंग

Type of word (Category):   Adjective

English meaning: sparkling or shining brightly

Hindi meaning: बहुत शानदार

Synonyms: sparkling, gleaming, dazzling, glinting, bright

Antonyms: dull, drab, dreary, dumb

English Example: Mira Rajput is looking scintillating in a picture shot by Shahid Kapoor.

Hindi Example: मीरा राजपूत शाहिद कपूर द्वारा ली गयी एक तस्वीर में बहुत शानदार दिख रही है।

WOD: *Iconic*

Pronunciation: आइकानिक

Type of word (Category):   Adjective

English meaning: very famous or popular, especially being considered to represent particular opinions or a particular time

Hindi meaning: प्रतिष्ठित

Synonyms: symbolic, famous, well-known, known

Antonyms: unrecognizable, unimportant, insignificant

English Example: India's first Madame Tussauds wax museum is now open for the public at the iconic Regal building in central Delhi.

Hindi Example: भारत का पहला मैडम तुसाइस वैक्स म्यूजियम अब जनता के लिए मध्य दिल्ली के प्रतिष्ठित रीगल भवन में खुला है।

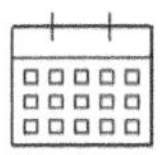 **Date: 2017/12/05**

WOD: *Toxic*

Pronunciation: टॉक्सिक

Type of word (Category): Adjective

English meaning: poisonous

Hindi meaning: विषाक्त

Synonyms: poisonous, venomous, virulent, noxious, malignant, pernicious

Antonyms: harmless, healthy, nonpoisonous, nontoxic

English Example: Delhi's toxic air halted the ongoing third Test between India and Sri Lanka for around 20 minutes on Sunday.

Hindi Example: दिल्ली की विषाक्त हवा ने भारत और श्रीलंका के बीच रविवार को हो रहे तीसरे टेस्ट को करीब 20 मिनट के लिए रोक दिया।

Date: 2017/12/06

WOD: *Exponent*

Pronunciation: इक्स्पोनन्ट

Type of word (Category): Noun

English meaning: a person who supports an idea or theory and tries to persuade people of its truth or benefits

Hindi meaning: प्रतिनिधि

Synonyms: advocate, supporter, proponent, upholder, propagandist

Antonyms: antagonist, opponent, adversary

English Example: Indian cinema has lost one of its greatest unsung exponents.

Hindi Example: भारतीय सिनेमा ने अपने सबसे बड़े अकीर्तित प्रतिनिधियों में से एक को खो दिया है।

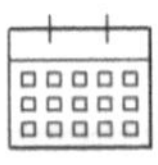 **Date: 2017/12/07**

WOD: *Nuptial*

Pronunciation: नप्शल

Type of word (Category):   Adjective

English meaning: relating to marriage or weddings

Hindi meaning: वैवाहिक

Synonyms: matrimonial, marital, conjugal, wedding, connubial

Antonyms: divorce

English Example: Bharti Singh and Haarsh Limbachiyaa finally took the nuptial vows in Goa.

Hindi Example: भारती सिंह और हर्ष लिंबाचिया ने आखिरकार गोवा में वैवाहिक वचन लिए।

Date: 2017/12/08

WOD: *Streak*

Pronunciation: स्ट्रीक

Type of word (Category):   Noun

English meaning: a continuous period of specified success or luck

Hindi meaning: दौर

Synonyms: period, spell, stretch, run, time

Antonyms: -

English Example: After winning test series against Sri Lanka, India has matched Australia's streak of nine consecutive series wins.

Hindi Example: श्रीलंका के खिलाफ टेस्ट सीरीज जीतने के बाद, भारत ने ऑस्ट्रेलिया के लगातार नौ श्रृंखला जीतने के दौर की बराबरी कर ली है।

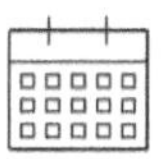 **Date: 2017/12/09**

WOD: *Weirdo*

Pronunciation: विर्डो

Type of word (Category):   Noun

English meaning: a person whose dress or behavior seems strange or eccentric

Hindi meaning: अजीब आदमी

Synonyms: eccentric, freak, crank, crazy, oddity, weirdie

Antonyms: normal, ordinary, typical

English Example: In Fukrey Returns, Varun Sharma as Choocha has played a role of weirdo who has superpowers to watch bizarre dreams.

Hindi Example: फुकरे रिटर्न्स में, वरुण शर्मा ने चूचा के रूप में एक अजीब आदमी की भूमिका निभाई है जिसमें विचित्र सपने देखने की अलौकिक शक्तियां है।

Date: 2017/12/10

WOD: *Mantle*

Pronunciation: मेन्टल

Type of word (Category):   Noun

English meaning: an important role or responsibility that passes from one person to another

Hindi meaning: दायित्व

Synonyms: role, duty, responsibility, position, job, onus

Antonyms: -

English Example: IT sectors have welcomed Infosys' decision to hand over the mantle to Salil Parekh.

Hindi Example: आईटी संस्थाओं ने सलिल पारेख को दायित्व सौंपने के इन्फोसिस के फैसले का स्वागत किया है।

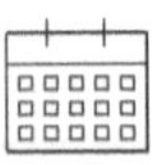 **Date: 2017/12/11**

WOD: *Flak*

Pronunciation: फ्लैक

Type of word (Category): Noun

English meaning: strong criticism

Hindi meaning: कड़ी आलोचना

Synonyms: criticism, condemnation, complaints, censure, denunciation

Antonyms: praise, compliment, support, approval

English Example: Hina Khan faced flak for her snide remarks on Sakshi Tanwar.

Hindi Example: साक्षी तंवर पर व्यंग्यात्मक टिप्पणियों के लिए हिना खान ने कड़ी आलोचना का सामना किया।

Date: 2017/12/12

WOD: *Elite*

Pronunciation: ऐ-लीट

Type of word (Category): Adjective

English meaning: belonging to the richest, most powerful, best-educated, or best-trained group in a society, selected as the best

Hindi meaning: सर्वोत्कृष्ट

Synonyms: best, exclusive, superior, supreme

Antonyms: worst, ordinary, common

English Example: India joined elite multilateral export control regime.

Hindi Example: भारत सर्वोत्कृष्ट बहुपक्षीय निर्यात नियंत्रण व्यवस्था में शामिल हुआ।

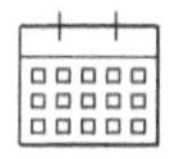 **Date: 2017/12/13**

WOD: *Hush hush*

Pronunciation: हश-हश

Type of word (Category): Adjective

English meaning: kept secret from people, highly secret or confidential

Hindi meaning: गोपनीय

Synonyms: confidential, secret, covert, private, hidden

Antonyms: public, revealed, known

English Example: Virat Kohli and Anushka Sharma tied the knot in a hush-hush ceremony in Italy.

Hindi Example: विराट कोहली और अनुष्का शर्मा इटली में एक गोपनीय समारोह में शादी के बंधन में बंध गए।

 **Date: 2017/12/14**

WOD: *Influential*

Pronunciation: इन्फ्लू-एन्शल

Type of word (Category): Adjective

English meaning: having great influence on someone or something

Hindi meaning: प्रभावशाली

Synonyms: powerful, authoritative, dominant, important, effective

Antonyms: unimportant, insignificant, ineffective

English Example: Rahul Gandhi became the sixth and the youngest president of the influential Congress party.

Hindi Example: राहुल गांधी प्रभावशाली कांग्रेस पार्टी के छठे और सबसे कम उम्र के अध्यक्ष बने।

 **Date: 2017/12/15**

WOD: *Belligerent*

Pronunciation: बे-लिजरन्ट

Type of word (Category): *Adjective*

English meaning: *inclined to or exhibiting assertiveness, hostility, or combativeness*

Hindi meaning: संघर्षपूर्ण

Synonyms: *aggressive, combative, bellicose, warring*

Antonyms: *friendly, peaceable, amicable*

English Example: *In a belligerent inning, Rohit Sharma hit 12 sixes and 13 fours to score his third double century.*

Hindi Example: एक संघर्षपूर्ण पारी में, रोहित शर्मा ने अपना तीसरा दोहरा शतक बनाने के लिए 12 छक्के और 13 चौके लगाए।

Date: 2017/12/16

WOD: *Flummoxed*

Pronunciation: फ्लमॉक्स्ट

Type of word (Category): *Adjective*

English meaning: *bewildered or perplexed*

Hindi meaning: भौंचक्का

Synonyms: *baffle, bewildered, mystify, bemuse, perplex, astounded*

Antonyms: *enlightened, explained*

English Example: *Congress leader Shashi Tharoor's extensive vocabulary has often made his Twitter followers flummoxed.*

Hindi Example: कांग्रेस नेता शशि थरूर की व्यापक शब्दावली उनके ट्विटर अनुयायियों को अक्सर भौंचक्का कर देती है।

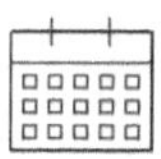

Date: 2017/12/17

WOD: *Replenish*

Pronunciation: रि-प्लेनिश

Type of word (Category):   *Verb*

English meaning: *fill (something) up again*

Hindi meaning: फिर से भरना

Synonyms: *refill, fill up, recharge, reload*

Antonyms: *damage, deplete, use up*

English Example: *The government has proposed that ATMs should not be replenished with cash after 9 pm in cities.*

Hindi Example: सरकार ने प्रस्ताव रखा है कि शहरों में 9 बजे के बाद एटीएम को नकदी से फिर से नहीं भरा जाना चाहिए।

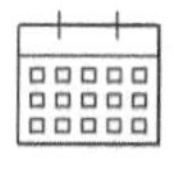

Date: 2017/12/18

WOD: *Predator*

Pronunciation: प्रेडटर

Type of word (Category):   *Noun*

English meaning: *an animal that naturally preys on others*

Hindi meaning: परभक्षी

Synonyms: *hunter, carnivore, vulture, beast of prey*

Antonyms: *prey, herbivore*

English Example: *The submarine INS Kalvari is named after the dreaded tiger shark, a deadly deep sea predator of the Indian Ocean.*

Hindi Example: पनडुब्बी आईएनएस कलवरी का नाम खतरनाक टाइगर शार्क पर रखा गया है, जो की हिंद महासागर के गहरे समुद्र का एक प्राणघातक परभक्षी है।

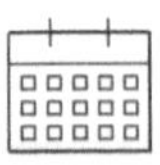 **Date: 2017/12/19**

WOD: *Ensure*

Pronunciation: इन्शुर

Type of word (Category): *Verb*

English meaning: *to make something certain to happen*

Hindi meaning: सुनिश्चित करना

Synonyms: *assure, secure, make certain, ascertain, insure*

Antonyms: *endanger, harm, deny, contradict*

English Example: *Spinners and Shikhar Dhawan ensured eight-wicket victory for India against Sri Lanka.*

Hindi Example: स्पिनरों और शिखर धवन ने श्रीलंका के खिलाफ भारत के लिए आठ विकेट से जीत सुनिश्चित की।

Date: 2017/12/20

WOD: *Legendary*

Pronunciation: लेजन्डेरी

Type of word (Category): *Adjective*

English meaning: *remarkable enough to be famous; very well known*

Hindi meaning: प्रसिद्ध

Synonyms: *famous, celebrated, renowned, acclaimed, venerable, notable*

Antonyms: *unknown, infamous, unimportant*

English Example: *Legendary actress Rekha was honoured with the Smita Patil Memorial Award in Mumbai.*

Hindi Example: प्रसिद्ध अभिनेत्री रेखा को मुंबई में स्मिता पाटिल मेमोरियल अवार्ड से सम्मानित किया गया।

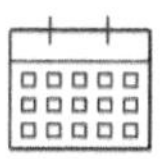 **Date: 2017/12/21**

WOD: *Ram*

Pronunciation: रेम

Type of word (Category):   Verb

English meaning: roughly force (something) into place

Hindi meaning: टक्कर मारना

Synonyms: clash, collide, hammer, bang, force

Antonyms: halt, stop

English Example: Driverless Delhi Metro train rammed into wall during trial.

Hindi Example: ड्रायवरलेस दिल्ली मेट्रो ट्रेन ने परीक्षण के दौरान दीवार में टक्कर मारी।

Date: 2017/12/22

WOD: *Ancestral*

Pronunciation: ऐन्सेस्ट्रल

Type of word (Category):   Adjective

English meaning: of, belonging to, or inherited from an ancestor or ancestors

Hindi meaning: पैतृक

Synonyms: hereditary, paternal, inherited, patriarchal, familial

Antonyms: adopted, filial

English Example: Taimur Ali Khan celebrated his first birthday at his ancestral home, the Pataudi Palace.

Hindi Example: तैमूर अली खान ने अपने पैतृक घर, पटौदी महल में अपना पहला जन्मदिन मनाया।

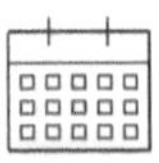 **Date: 2017/12/23**

WOD: *Amid*

Pronunciation: अ-मिड

Type of word (Category):   Preposition

English meaning: surrounded by; in the middle of

Hindi meaning: के बीच

Synonyms: among, between, surrounded by, amidst, amongst

Antonyms: outside, beyond, away from

English Example: India tested anti-smog gun in Delhi amid heavy air pollution.

Hindi Example: भारी वायु प्रदूषण के बीच भारत ने दिल्ली में एंटी-स्मॉग गन का परीक्षण किया।

Date: 2017/12/24

WOD: *Riveting*

Pronunciation: रिवेटिंग

Type of word (Category):   Adjective

English meaning: extremely interesting

Hindi meaning: दिलचस्प

Synonyms: fascinating, engrossing, interesting, gripping, captivating

Antonyms: boring, tedious, uninteresting, monotonous

English Example: The riveting chemistry between Tiger and Zoya in 'Tiger Zinda Hai' movie has enchanted the audience.

Hindi Example: टाइगर जिंदा है' फिल्म में टाइगर और जोया के बीच की दिलचस्प केमिस्ट्री ने दर्शकों को मंत्रमुग्ध किया है।

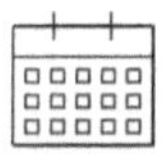 **Date: 2017/12/25**

WOD: *Maestro*

Pronunciation: माइस्ट्रो

Type of word (Category): *Noun*

English meaning: *a distinguished figure in any sphere*

Hindi meaning: माहिर

Synonyms: *virtuoso, master, expert, genius*

Antonyms: *tyro, beginner*

English Example: *Cricket maestro Sachin Tendulkar on Thursday could not give his maiden speech in the Rajya Sabha amid uproar.*

Hindi Example: गुरुवार को क्रिकेट के माहिर सचिन तेंदुलकर शोरगुल के बीच राज्यसभा में अपना पहला भाषण नहीं दे सके।

Date: 2017/12/26

WOD: *Gaze*

Pronunciation: गेज़

Type of word (Category): *Noun*

English meaning: *a steady intent look*

Hindi meaning: निगाह

Synonyms: *stare, look, sight, view, glare*

Antonyms: -

English Example: *Rani Mukerji wants to keep her daughter away from media gaze.*

Hindi Example: रानी मुखर्जी अपनी बेटी को मीडिया की निगाह से दूर रखना चाहती हैं।

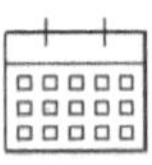
Date: 2017/12/27

WOD: *Sojourn*

Pronunciation: सॉजॅःन

Type of word (Category): Noun

English meaning: a temporary stay

Hindi meaning: अस्थाई निवास

Synonyms: stay, stop, visit, brief travel, stopover

Antonyms: reside

English Example: On December 28, Indian cricket team is going for almost two-month long sojourn in South Africa.

Hindi Example: 28 दिसंबर को, भारतीय क्रिकेट टीम दक्षिण अफ्रीका में लगभग दो महीने के लंबे अस्थाई निवास के लिए जा रही है।

Date: 2017/12/28

WOD: *Fanfare*

Pronunciation: फैन्फेर

Type of word (Category): Noun

English meaning: a gaudy outward display, media attention or elaborate ceremony

Hindi meaning: धूमधाम

Synonyms: splendour, display, ostentation, publicity

Antonyms: hiding, concealment

English Example: Mumbai welcomed with great fanfare its first air-conditioned local train.

Hindi Example: मुंबई ने बड़े धूमधाम के साथ अपनी पहली वातानुकूलित लोकल ट्रेन का स्वागत किया।

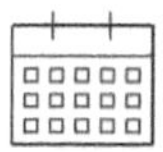 **Date: 2017/12/29**

WOD: *Delectable*

Pronunciation: डिलेक्टबॅल

Type of word (Category): Adjective

English meaning: extremely attractive

Hindi meaning: बहुत आकर्षक

Synonyms: delightful, lovely, captivating, appealing

Antonyms: horrible, unattractive

English Example: Viswanathan Anand of India defeated current champion Magnus Carlsen in a delectable game.

Hindi Example: भारत के विश्वनाथन आनंद ने एक बहुत आकर्षक खेल में मौजूदा चैंपियन मैग्नस कार्ल्सन को हराया।

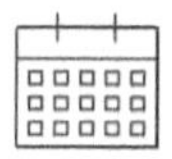 **Date: 2017/12/30**

WOD: *Devastating*

Pronunciation: डिवस्टेटिंग

Type of word (Category): Adjective

English meaning: extremely highly destructive or damaging

Hindi meaning: भयानक

Synonyms: destructive, ruinous, disastrous, fatal, deadly

Antonyms: blessed, fortunate

English Example: A devastating fire broke out at Mumbai's Kamala Mills on Friday night.

Hindi Example: शुक्रवार रात मुंबई के कमला मिल्स में भयानक आग लग गई।

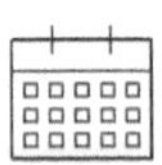

WOD: *Withdraw*

Pronunciation: विद्ड्रॉ

Type of word (Category): *Verb*

English meaning: *to take or move out or back, or to remove*

Hindi meaning: वापस लेना

Synonyms: *lift, draw back, reverse, rescind, repeal*

Antonyms: *introduce, bring in, maintain*

English Example: *The Centre has withdrawn its decision to raise LPG prices by Rs. 4 a cylinder every month.*

Hindi Example: केंद्र ने एलपीजी की कीमतें हर महीने 4 रुपये प्रति सिलेंडर बढ़ाए जाने के अपने फैसले को वापस ले लिया है।

Namaste **Hindi**

Learning Hindi is fun now

- Offline mode
- 100 + Lesson
- Learn Hindi from Game
- Learn Hindi from Conversation

Scan QR code
to download the App

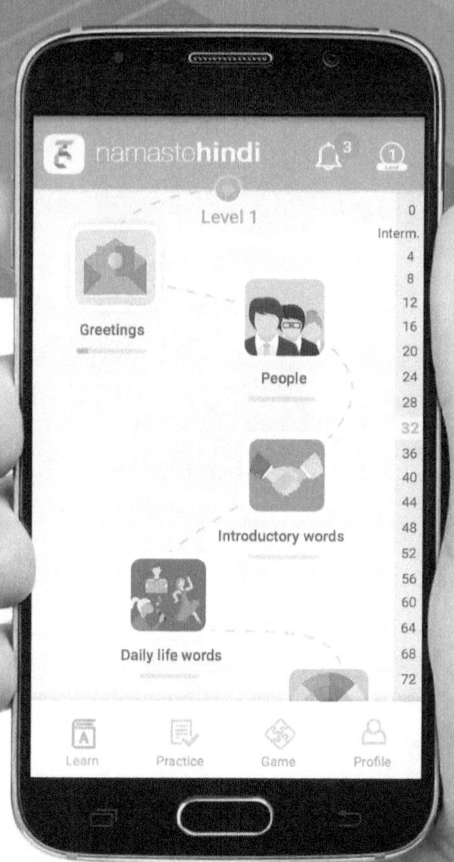